D1544827

NC

# Northern Pike

# Northern Pike

WILL RYAN

The Lyons Press

10   9   8   7   6   5   4   3   2   1

Printed in the United States of America

Library of Congress Cataloging-in-Publication Data
Ryan, Will, 1951–
   Northern pike/Will Ryan.
     p.   cm.
   Includes bibliographical references (p.).
   ISBN 1-58574-044-6
   1. Pike. 2. Pike fishing. I. Title.

 SH691.P6 R93 2000
 799.1'759—dc21                                                                              99-054423

# Contents

# ACKNOWLEDGMENTS

As I wrote on a previous occasion, media often portray authors as snooty and superior, but writing a book is a humbling undertaking.

A number of people have been very helpful to me along the way. Hampshire College students Alyssa Bennet, Mark Feltskog, and in particular Ryan Kerney offered invaluable research assistance. Members of various fisheries departments—Al Schiavonne and Steve LaPan from the Region 6 DEC in New York State, John Hall from the Vermont Fish and Wildlife Department, Bill Hyatt from the Connecticut Fish and Wildlife Department, and Pete Mirick from the Massachusetts Division of Fisheries and Wildlife—have always taken time from busy days to answer my questions.

My friends at Hampshire College have been very helpful, too. Mark Feinstein and Steve Weisler helped me sort out issues in animal cognition. Aaron Berman, David Kerr, Bob Rakoff, and Mary Russo have been helpful in discussions of how humans construct an idea of wilderness. I've learned a good deal about writing from teaching with others at Hampshire, including Deb Gorlin, Lynne Hanley, Paul Jenkins, Michael Lesy, Robin Lewis, Nina Payne, Tamuira Reid, Ellie Siegel, Lamaretta Simmons, and Anna Sussman. I am particularly indebted to Ray Coppinger and Stan Warner, and could not have written this book without their assistance. They provided numerous photos and angling insights, say nothing of humor and good fellowship in the boat. As a wildlife biologist, Ray has contributed more than he knows to my understanding of fish and people; Stan, for his part, has never said "I told you so" after a failed expedition. Both bring an unmatched passion to the pursuit of pike.

When you're completing a manuscript, small kindnesses become immensely important, and my friends in the sporting press have certainly risen to this occasion—extending deadlines, returning photos before they're due, commiserating about a writer's lot, sending along an e-mail joke, or simply setting a date to go fishing. Ben Ardito, Jim Babb, Crispin Battles, Jim Butler, Matt Crawford, Jamus Driscoll, Tom Fuller, Ron Kolodziej, Bob McNitt, Frank Miniter, Ed Scheff, Mark Scott, Ralph Stuart, Bill Tapply, Mike Toth, and Tony Zappia have in all cases done as much and more.

The Lyons Press staff have been invaluable. Jay Cassell deftly smoothed out some of the manuscript's rough spots; David Klausmeyer ferreted out the more embarrassing mistakes; Laura Matteau copyedited with thoroughness and precision; and Jonathan McCullough kept the whole operation running. Dick Talleur's work with the color plates is exquisite. Nick Lyons lived up to his reputation as the patron saint of fishing writers, sending books, giving sage advice, maintaining his enthusiasm for pike. His counsel on the manuscript and project in general has been indispensable.

Most of my fishing friends would just as soon be angling for other species, so I want to thank them for their tolerance: Don Bechaz, Pete Bellinger, Bob Charlebois, the late Steve Charles, Mark Craig, Ted Creighton, Lee Ellsworth, Frank Flack, Morgan Grant, Shawn Gregoire, Scott Johnson, Jack LaHair, Kurt Lanning, the late Buzz LaRose, Ken Leon, Chris Loftus, Pete Loftus, Eugene Mancini, the late Dave Nolan, Ralph Ringer, Marcel Rocheleau, the late Ron "Tate" Tatro, and Todd Wheeler.

Most of all, I need to thank Noreen and Brody—you guys are great; you mean the world to me.

Mom and Dad, you're the ones who got me started with this mess. That is why this book, like the last one, is dedicated to you.

# Introduction

A few years ago the international wire services carried the story of a Russian ice fisherman and a pike he snaked out of an Asian lake in midwinter. Maybe he was showing off for his buddies. Maybe he'd seen a famous American bass fisherman offer a PDA to a prizewinning catch on television. Or maybe it just doesn't get any slower than a slow day of ice fishing in Russia. Whatever the reason, he was so overcome by his catch that he gave the pike a kiss, which prompted the pike to reciprocate by clamping down directly on his schnozz.

The pike claimed quite a bit of nose in its teeth, and the guy's comrades couldn't pry apart its jaws, try as they might. The angler landed in a hospital, where the pike was "surgically removed."

I imagine the AP ran this piece because of its reversal—the "fish eats fisherman" angle. Several friends who don't fish told me about the story, each smiling, implying that it spoke volumes about fishermen. Pike fishermen, of course, know better. I told several of them about the news item, and they laughed, too. To them the story spoke volumes about pike.

Pike inhabit a slimy, reptilian skin, and they come equipped with toothy jaws that click when they close. A pike is not the kind of fish you kiss—ever. Even a peck on the snout. Euphoric or not, the Russian should have known better.

On some level he probably did. It's just that pike are so easy to underestimate. Sometimes you can haul them in like a clump of seaweed and watch them loll at boatside, placid as a possum. A baleful eye rests on the waterline, leering back at you.

Funny how easily this pike came in. Too easily! The pike explodes, zips beneath the engine prop, and that's it. A fish story.

Pike certainly give birth to some wild ones. Most fish behave themselves in a boat. Oh, they might wiggle or flop as they're being unhooked, but that's about it. But pike invariably dump the tackle boxes, slime the sandwiches, and spill the beer. Having a "green" pike on board is like hosting a ferret in your long johns. Nobody's happy about where they are. When someone tells of a big trout or bass, it usually involves something the angler did to the fish. Fooled it, caught it, lost it, or whatever. When someone tells of a big pike, the gist of the tale almost invariably involves something the pike did. Smashed a plug, ate a walleye, nailed a duckling. French angler Pierre Affre tells of seeing a pike take a pheasant after it had been shot and fallen into the river. Just last winter a junior editor from one of the country's major outdoor magazines told me of seeing a pike attack a human. No joke.

"You know, when I was in summer camp in the Adirondack Mountains," he recalled, "one of the other campers got bit by a pike."

"What happened?"

"We were all in canoes, and this kid had been trailing his hand in the water and a pike swam up and bit his fingers. I saw the kid on shore. His hand was bleeding and the counselors were bandaging him up."

"That's pretty unusual. I don't believe there's a documented pike attack on record. Maybe it was a snapping turtle or a sharp rock."

"It was a pike. There were witnesses."

I found myself searching for a rejoinder but none came, and in the end was grateful for the chance to witness pike mythology in the making. Like sausage, the production can be a little unsettling, even if the end product comes to us as a full-flavored bit of life, spicy and delicious. We've been grinding out these pike stories for thousands of years.

Fishing for pike evokes similar hyperbole, as can be seen from the past and present inclination to exaggerate everything about them. Often as not they are the biggest fish in the bay or pond. They strike suddenly, and that, too, preys on fishermen, never ones to shy from tacking a few pounds onto the fish they might have caught. I know. A big pike glares down from the wall of many North Country barrooms. I've studied those fish many evenings, and none of them was anywhere near the size of the ones I've lost.

Trout, bass, walleyes, and such fish have routines, preferred forage, and ways of behaving, but pike defy prediction. Sometimes indifferent to lures or even human presence, pike at other times descend upon a bait or lure with a water-flying flourish

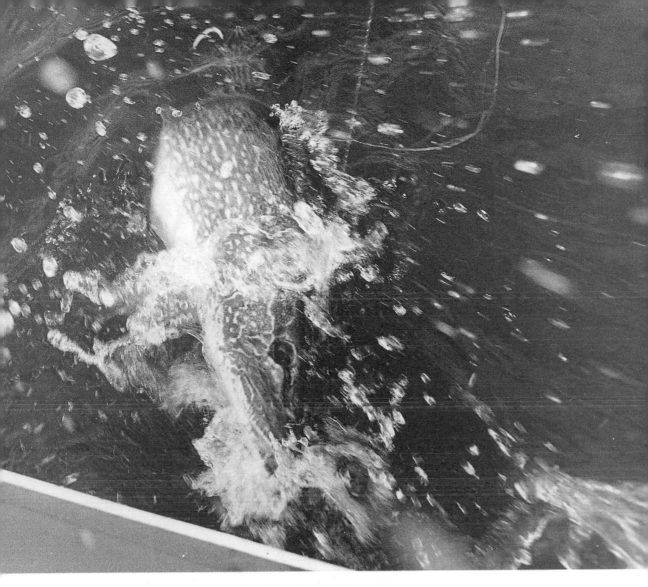

*A pike at boatside. Watch your fingers.*

that surprises with its fury. They are pre-suburban, belonging instead to a 19th-century wildness. A pike in your pond? You may as well have a wolf in your woodlot.

Attitudes about northerns follow larger historical and cultural patterns of humans and predators. Anglers who live in the heart of pike country fish for them most intensively through the ice and have less interest in them as sport fish. States in the southern part of the pike's range propagate and release pike in hopes of establishing fisheries. Massachusetts, for example, has continued a stocking program for more than 20 years even though actual reproduction is virtually nil. Anglers kill to catch them.

Today, interest in pike seems to be growing. We now know that they pose little threat to walleyes and trout, at least in comparison with the overall health of the ecosystem. Anglers no longer see it as their civic duty to cuss and destroy every pike they encounter. If anything, the pike's status within the angling community has never been higher, as an increasing number of anglers actually target northerns and articles and books on how to catch them proliferate. The fly-fishing community has discovered a new frontier of wilderness pike experiences, and that has also spurred interest in them. Local pike organizations—Pikers in Massachusetts and Northerns, Inc., in Minnesota, to name a couple—indicate clear enthusiasm. Pikemasters, a Michigan-based national organization dedicated to the conservation and propagation of northern pike, claims 1,000 members. So perhaps the time is right for a new look at northern pike.

I write mostly about the pike you can drive to, and I should tell you that right now. I'll certainly try to evoke the thrill of fishing the Canadian wilderness and outline the gear and tactics you'll need for that sort of angling. But I've always thought that articles and books dwell to excess on wilderness situations and ignore the problems pike anglers encounter in the northern United States and southern Canada. There's just a tremendous difference between fishing for a 30-pound pike that has never seen a lure and a 30-incher that sees Lord knows how many every day.

I can't guarantee this book will help you catch that nervous 30-incher, but I'm confident you'll come to understand that fish in a new way. My portrait of pike proceeds seasonally from winter through spring, summer, and fall. Pike are active in each season, are pursued by anglers in every month of the year: To overlook this dimension is to miss their essential nature, say nothing of their relationship with humans.

I have captured pike in every way imaginable, but this book sticks to tip-ups, bait, spinners, spoons, plastics, plugs, jigs, and flies. I look at new methods, but I hope I do justice by pike tradition in the process. My aim, in either case, is to apply various strategies to the fishing problems that unfold through the year.

I rely heavily on the scientific research on northern pike, of which there is plenty. The library's repositories of books and sporting magazines have helped me better understand the pike's social construction, too. I make liberal use of my lifelong experiences of fishing for them in the northern United States, as well as in Ontario and Quebec, and my hope is that these two avenues—the empirical and the experiential—together create a fresh perspective on a fine fish.

Though I have spent several years working on this book, I can honestly say that I do not figure fishing time into that accounting. I have fished for pike since childhood for the immense pleasure that the experience brings, for the opportunity to participate in their myths. Wiser anglers than I have noted the desultory results of using fishing time for something other than indulgence, and their caution has left me free to spend my time afloat with no agenda other than trailing my fingers in the water.

That continues to be an exhilarating undertaking. Pike lakes, it turns out, are full of surprises.

*The pike you can drive to.*

# PART I

## Winter, Early Spring

# 1

# Through the Ice

Winter across pike range is no passing fancy. It is a chopping, plowing, pipe-freezing, four-month affair beginning with January's procession of blizzards and arctic air masses. By midmonth the freezer door slams shut on North Country lakes. In this respect, a first peek at the pike waters of North America reveals nothing more than an infinite expanse of ice and snow, bereft of life.

It's a different universe beneath the ice, where pike slip through the thin weeds of winter, on the prowl. Northerns remain active over a wide range of water temperatures, from 32 to 70 degrees Fahrenheit. The biggest fish prefer water temperatures at the lower end of the range, so they spend much of the year in deep water. But when ice seals in their world, they return to the shallows where forage fish school. The ice, in effect, creates a controlled environment. Protected from wind, the water clarifies and its temperature stabilizes. Hunting could not be better.

As for us, the anglers, there's more to ice fishing than might be evident at first glance. Catching big pike through the ice involves a fair amount of skill, to say nothing of considerable suffering, for the harsh weather makes fierce demands. Yes, you can legally fish through a hole in the ice during a blizzard, but that doesn't make it the thinking man's move. There's no law against do-it-yourself dentistry, either.

## SAFE AND WARM

How much ice is enough? Standard guidelines insist on a minimum of 2 inches for one person, 3 inches for small groups in single file, and 4 or 5 inches for any number.

I like a little more hard stuff than that. Those measurements assume solid ice that, with springs, snow cover, and so forth, should never be assumed. You can drill or spud a test hole near shore if no other anglers greet you—though ice can be 5 inches thick in one spot, 2 inches in another. There may be a reason why no one else is on the ice. I wait for the crowds, for half a foot of good ice. It's not like winter's going anywhere.

*A bright mid-winter day on the ice gives hope through the long winters in pike country.*

Frozen lakes offer little in the way of protection, and it's the wind that's the devil. The ice-fishing shanty, which has been around for eons, can make the polar breezes bearable. Portable nylon wind blocks offer little in the way of nostalgia but plenty in the way of protection, which does wonders for morale.

Whatever you wait in (or behind), ice fishing consists of moments of exertion and hours of waiting, usually for more exertion. It makes sense to bring along plenty of food, as well as a heavy parka and mittens. When you're towing gear, drilling holes, and setting lines, you don't need that final heavy layer. When the work is done, you'll be glad you brought it along.

Experienced anglers pay attention to certain areas of the body, namely the extremities. A warm cap that covers your ears is a must. I bring two pairs of mittens: a big pair for warming and a smaller, more flexible pair for fishing. Modern insulated liners and boots make it easy—or at least easier than it used to be—to keep your feet warm. However, I still use a trick my dad taught me years ago: Just before going, wash your feet in cool water. That inhibits sweating, which is how feet get cold. On the way to ice fishing, wear light cotton socks and shoes so your feet don't perspire in the warm truck. Upon arrival at the ice, slip on the insulated socks and big boots. Your feet won't always stay toasty warm, but at least they won't be the first parts of your body to freeze. Finally, you need to protect your face from windburn and sunburn; bright days in late February can zap your skin.

## EQUIPMENT

The first time I spudded through 3 feet of ice, I gained new respect for old-time ice fishermen. The modern screw-type auger is a wonderful labor-saving advance. If you go every weekend, you may want to invest in a gas auger, which zips through 2 feet of ice like it's butter. Either way, get the 8-inch bit. You'll need a sled to drag your gear across the ice, a skimmer to keep your holes open, a bucket and net for bait, a sounder and assorted buttons to determine and mark depth, and hooks, sinkers, and leaders.

Terminal tackle depends upon how you intend to fish, but most pike anglers set at least some tip-ups or tilts. The tip-up is the original automatic fisherman. You can imagine its origin, almost see an old Yankee angler inside a shanty, looking out and saying, "Gawwdammit, it's cold out there, and warm in here. Now if I had me something that would . . ."

The tip-up looks a little like an old-fashioned coat and hat rack. At its center is a wooden stake, to the top of which is attached a wire adorned with a bright orange square of plastic; a spool of line is affixed to the bottom of the stake, and four legs sprout from its midsection to form a brace across the ice hole so that the spool rests beneath the water surface and the orange flag waits, poised to spring into the air. The tip-up is set by bending the wire and flag into a loop and fastening it to a wire catch partway down the stake. The spool holds the minnow-baited hook just above the weeds. When a pike runs with the minnow, the spool turns, triggering the wire catch on the stake, which lets the flag spring to life.

You can spend quite a bit of money on tip-ups, and they all do pretty much the same thing. The original design is a bit of North Country genius that modifications haven't improved as much as their price tags suggest. In general, bigger spools snarl less frequently, and new models don't ice up or give you as many wind flags to chase. The expensive tip-ups feel less rickety, but it's not like you're driving one to Florida. The whole matter is a lot like augers—if you fish every weekend, spend the money.

## SETTING UP

My cousin Don Bechaz, a dairy farmer who lives in upstate New York, goes after northerns quite a bit in the winter. Once he's finished with the morning milking, he often heads down to the St. Lawrence River ice shack he shares with his friend Pete Ledoux. A woodstove and ice holes in the floorboards mean you can jerk perch and watch your tip-ups through the window—all in your shirtsleeves. The smoke gets a little thick sometimes, but you can just open the door and air things out.

Don and Pete are nothing if not the relaxed angling team, but as I've come to realize, they have a meticulous side as well. I'd fished with Don all my life, mostly in spring and summer for bullheads and bass, and had never known him to take fishing all that seriously. In the family his prowess as an angler rests on his reputation for practical jokes, for things like lighting the cherry bomb *just* as you're fishing the bullhead out of the mud.

So I was unprepared for the bits of exactitude that emerged on our first ice-fishing trip back in the late 1970s, when I was just starting to winter fish for pike. I had my tip-ups set and was back in the shanty eating myself into oblivion; meanwhile, Don was still working on his rigs, and I waddled over to get a closer look.

"What's going on?" I asked.

"Sounding," he said, "and the weeds don't have a constant height. There, I think that's the top." He moved his button down to mark it. "I'll put this one a foot above the grass," he continued, moving the button down some 12 inches to add another half foot. "For the spool being beneath the ice," he said, anticipating my question.

Don was using a 3-foot, 17-pound-test monofilament leader to which he'd attached a 12-inch wire leader with a size 1 snelled hook. A single split shot provided weight. He selected a minnow, baited his hook, and carefully set the tip-up in the hole—as if returning an antique to the shelf.

"Both suckers and shiners work," Don explained, breath smoking in the January air. "I think shiners make a better bait because they act nervous in the water. I want my bait fishing if I'm gonna be waiting. You know what I mean? I like them in the 4- to 6-inch range. Some days it matters; other days the pike will hit anything, even perch minnows."

Most anglers use terminal gear similar to Don's: a 4- to 8-inch shiner, chub, or sucker; a button or tiny bobber as a depth marker; a 3-foot leader of 15- to 30-pound-test with a foot-long wire leader; and a light sinker and size 1 or 1/0 hook. Treble hooks give a better set, though I find the single hook easier to extract. A quick-strike harness, which involves two hooks that stretch along the bait, removes the guesswork from setting the hook, if you're so inclined.

Personally, I like watching the spool spin and find the struggle to maintain judgment while the line disappears to be a reason in itself to ice fish for northerns. It helps to turn the spool so that the line unwinds directly toward the running fish (rather than looping off the side). This maneuver eases drag on the line and limits the likelihood of snarls. Conventional wisdom calls for letting the pike run until it stops, then starts again. The problem with this approach is twofold. First, the longer the pike runs, the greater the chance of your split shot ticking on weeds or logs, which can cause the fish to drop the bait. Second, such a pike has almost certainly swallowed the hook. In the past this was never much of a concern, but it is (or should be) today. The compromise position is to hit the pike at 15 to 20 feet, which results in as many hook-ups as the other methods.

To set the hook, kneel down and lift the tip-up from the water, then place it to one the side with the spool off the ice so that line can still run. Try to remain slightly back from the hole, so you can coil line in front of you as you take it in. That way, you'll have some easy-access untangled line if the fish is a big one. Gather line until you feel the "aliveness" of the fish on the other end; this doesn't take much delicacy if the line is melting from the spool, but may require a gentle touch if the pike has stopped. Grasp the line near the edge of the water and draw back sharply. This direct connection to the fish enjoys no cushion, no elasticity. It's a bit like playing tug-of-war with a frisky retriever. Old sweaters break before ice-fishing line, which frequently tests at 36 pounds (most leaders at least 20), so you want to keep the pressure on the fish.

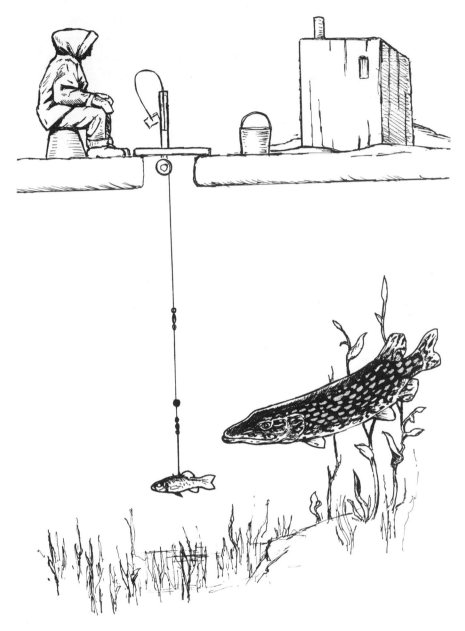

*It's important to set tip-ups along a drop-off, and "sound" first so that the minnow is above the weeds.*

Most pike escape at the last moment. Take your time, keep up pressure, and try to "ice" the pike with a sweep rather than popping it out with a jerk. Determine the pike's fate before landing it, as northerns have sensitive gills that can freeze in the wind. If you release the fish, do so immediately.

## JIG FISHING

Pike will take a jig and minnow quite readily. For years I caught an occasional pike in this fashion incidentally, while jigging for perch. Then I read an article in *New York Sportsman* by Paul Keesler. I was fascinated to read his description of using jigs to catch northerns intentionally. Paul was right. A light ice rod, 6-pound test (and wire leader), and a Swedish Pimple tipped with a 4-inch shiner made the perfect combination for working the shallow weed edges and simulating open-water fishing.

*Jig fishing with a minnow and Swedish Pimple is an increasingly popular strategy.*

In recent years many anglers have begun jigging pike through the ice in this fashion. Common sense suggests its effectiveness: Think how many strikes come when you're setting or pulling tip-ups. If states further curtail the number of tip-ups allowed, jigging will no doubt increase. Sitting around watching a single tip-up can leave even the most enthusiastic angler feeling a little foolish.

In general, you have a slimmer chance at a trophy by jigging, but then I'm not a trophy seeker. I find it more fun hooking and playing smaller fish on a rod than holding out for a larger fish on a handline. Of course, you do miss a lot of the discussion in the ice shanty when you're out jigging. In the end I usually manage to squeeze in some of both.

Spoon and minnow combinations are the most common rigs. Some anglers use dead smelt that have been frozen and rig them with quick-strike harnesses. Dead smelt apparently exude a strong scent. Though pike are visual hunters, the scent can't hurt, particularly since you are working and reworking the same patch of water.

## ICE-FISHING SEASONS

Weather above the ice affects the fish beneath it. I'll never forget one gloomy, midwinter morning on the St. Lawrence River near Ogdensburg, New York, back in the early 1980s. My friend Peter Mirick and I had driven over from Massachusetts the evening before and we were revved up, rain or not. But first we had to pry my old fishing buddy Pete Bellinger, our local "guide," from his living room couch. You are usually talking Jaws of Life for this sort of job, but we persevered.

Outside the gloom deepened, and a steady drizzle began. Bellinger was all for a rain check as we lingered over breakfast at the local grease pit. I wasn't far behind. "Best fishing is when the water's running right in the hole," Mirick said. He'd driven for seven hours, in rain, sleet, fog, and snow, dodging snowplows, slaloming through stranded vehicles. He'd never caught a pike through the ice. There was no choice.

We pulled on waders and rain gear and hit the ice. The pike bit like they were trying out new teeth, and they kept us splishing and splashing, running after flags all morning. Around 11 A.M. the rain turned to sleet, and we forgot about the bath. Flags popped faster than we could set tip-ups. Then sleet became snow; the wind shifted to the northwest and came whisking down from Canada. We began experimenting with new skin colors. And the pike? It was like you'd flipped a switch—party over.

One of angling's little mysteries. Why do fish bite so much better before a front or when it's a few degrees warmer? The water temperature clearly doesn't change. But

*Last ice fishing means hip boots and careful attention to conditions of ice.*

winter pike become increasingly active just before a storm—just as they do during the summer.

It may seem curious to think of ice fishing having seasons. After all, whether mid-January or mid-March, it's still water beneath the ice. But in fact pike behavior and location change considerably over the course of a winter. As experienced anglers know, the first few weeks of solid ice offer fast action as northerns invade the shallows and hold along the inside of weedlines in 2 to 10 feet of water. Pike move deeper as winter strengthens its grip and the shallows lose their weed growth. Look for northerns outside deeper weedlines in 10, 15, even 20 feet of water. My friends Pete and Chris Loftus fish deep on the outside edges of big open bays on eastern Lake Ontario during this midwinter period. They don't catch any more than four or five fish per day, but they sure win more than their share of local fishing derbies. As they explain it, moving into shallower water would definitely up their numbers of fish, but it would also reduce the size of the ones they catch.

As days become longer in late February, pike move back into shallow bays near spawning areas, which are usually swampy inlets, flooded timber stands, or marshy backwaters. Most anglers begin the month on the 15-foot weed shelf and end up working the 5-foot depths as winter wanes.

This pre-spawn period offers the best chance to catch big northerns. Some anglers specialize in this situation, and they consider a strike per day good fishing. Dedicated trophy hunters deliberately seek out oligotrophic waters or reservoirs with little cover, where pike are few but grow big. They go there as late as the season and ice conditions allow. Some use dead smelt that have been frozen and rigged with quick-strike harnesses, but large (12- to 15-inch) suckers remain the top choice.

These anglers bring camping gear, cribbage boards, and plenty of wood for the stove. They're in it for the long haul. If you haven't noticed, the same ones catch eye-popping pike every year. They take their vacation in March, and they aren't going to Aruba.

## ICE FISHING AS SPORT

Catching these big northerns may not be the most genteel of outdoor pursuits. Neither is the Iditarod, for that matter, but that doesn't make it less of a race.

My Vermont friends Lee Winchester and Tom Mason are out the door in the middle of the night and setting up by flashlight. It's a weird scene, that predawn life of trophy ice fishermen. I remember one time standing in line waiting for bait at 4 A.M. in a dank basement, a single lightbulb dangling from a wire. The guy who owned the basement was standing in front of two tubs, one filled with suckers, one with smelt. He was smoking a cigar, amply filling out a T-shirt, and selling bait as fast as he could count the money (though, as my friend Marcel later noted, winter is a pretty short season if you're in retail). I was the designated bait buyer; the others waited outside with station wagon running.

"I don't know what to buy," the guy in front of me said, as the line moved ahead a step. We waited with our empty buckets. "The suckers are cheaper and probably give you a better bait, but you can eat the smelt at the end of the day if the pike don't get 'em first." He gave me a wink. Then I realized he was serious.

"My wife wants me to bring some fish home to eat," he added, appearing rather pleased with himself. "With the smelt, you can't lose."

I have a friend in Florida who always asks, "What the hell do you do up there all winter, anyway?" He should catch this scene.

Or check out the enthusiasm ice fishermen bring to the ice and the resulting full-day wait for a flag to spring. Interestingly, Mason, Winchester, and other Vermonters call tip-ups "traps." This makes sense. Whether you're ice fishing or fur trapping, you bait up, set the "trap" for the proper depth in front of a likely lair, and wait. With so little under control, it's small wonder that ice fishermen exact a precise approach to those things they can control, even hedging bets on bringing home fish for dinner.

Mason and Winchester usually don't spend the night in their shack, but it has been known to happen. The wait, oddly, becomes a preliminary part of the excitement. There's so little sign of life that a strike attains a singular intensity when one finally does come. You look out over the same field of unsprung tip-ups time and again, realizing full well that they are iced over. Time to check them? You decide against it for a while, look once more, and the flag is up! You scurry over, sliding, and as you approach the hole, you hear the most welcome sound in all of ice fishing—the faint rattle of a spinning spool.

I remember several years ago fishing the St. Lawrence near Clayton with Lee Ellsworth, Pete Bellinger, my cousin Don, Pete Ledoux, and Chris and Pete Loftus. It was a brutal day, gray and cold with blowing snow. We were having fun simply by virtue of not having to endure it. Inside the shanty the stove glowed. We had some venison stew and a beer or two.

"Getting a little fogged up in here. I can hardly see my tip-ups," Don said. He wiped the glass and squinted out the ice shanty window. "Hey, there's a flag now!" Don lurched to his feet and burst from the shanty. He shuffled aross the ice toward the brave little patch of orange shivering in the wind on the outside edge of the tip-ups. The rest of us hesitated in the teeth of the subzero breeze, then fell out of the shanty almost in a line.

Don is a confirmed fast striker, which is why we hurried to his tip-up. He'd already hooked the fish by the time we reached the hole. A minute or two later he slid a fat pike out through the ice hole. It was a good one—7, maybe 8 pounds.

"Four-pounder, easy," Ledoux said.

"Why, you . . ." Don stopped and looked at his fish, at us, and back at the fish, which he'd gripped across the back with a hand that was quickly becoming cherry red in the breeze. He had a grin as wide as the river channel, as bright as the promise of spring.

## CONSERVATION

The ice-fishing decoys you see in museums speak of another approach to ice fishing, that done with a spear. At one time common throughout pike range, spearing today is limited to select waters in Wisconsin, Michigan, and Minnesota.

*Small pike are vulnerable to ice fishing. Lee Ellsworth.*

The trick was (and still is) to draw the pike within range by lowering beneath the ice a wooden or metal decoy of some sort—usually representing a sucker, trout, or pike. The decoy is weighted so you can fasten line to a top loop and swim it in circles, which in turn attracts the attention of any pike in the neighborhood. The angler-hunter waits, spear poised, as the pike approaches the decoy for close inspection. The darkened house in effect brightens the world beneath the ice. The spear is heavily weighted so it can be thrown through the depths in case the pike remains out of reach.

By today's standards of sporting gear and fair chase, the spear seems barbaric. I've never speared a fish through the ice, but I have done so in open water in spring, and I can sense its appeal. There's something most deliberate about spearing a fish; it is not at all like setting a hook and sitting back and playing a fish. Spearing really is closer to hunting in that you aim, then propel your weapon, and strive for that odd—some would say, perverse—sense of connection with your prey.

Not surprisingly, spearing is controversial. Defenders say they can select their quarry; opponents say that's just the point—they take the bigger ones. Either way, the debate reflects the larger vulnerability of northerns through the ice and the fact that the one time you hear much about them is during the winter when, for two months a year, all the other fish are out of reach. That's when people start worrying about pike as gamefish.

Where I fish on Lake Ontario and the St. Lawrence River, nearly every town sponsors a derby. Good for the local economy, winter social event, and so forth. That's the good news. The bad news is that anglers kill a lot of 5-pound pike.

Ice-fishing pressure can have a clear effect on the size of the pike in a small body of water. The big fish can get caught out rather quickly. Does ice fishing have a com-

*All pike that will be returned require careful handling.*

parable effect on bigger bodies of water? Some, perhaps. People often say ice-fishing pressure explains the small size of the northerns in the St. Lawrence River and Lake Champlain. But these fish have historically been small, and the bays of Lake Ontario get just as much pressure and have fish that grow bigger.

Of course, ice-fishing pressure doesn't do any pike fishery any good. Careful handling is key (not kicking the fish or grabbing them by the eyes, for example). I asked Steve LaPan, New York State DEC Region 6 fisheries biologist, about the impact of ice fishing. He said: "Certainly the data from Perch Lake [a small, shallow lake that is open to ice fishing only] show that ice fishing can have an impact on a small fishery. As for big waters like Lake Ontario and the St. Lawrence River, there's no evidence that ice fishing has any significant effect on the overall fishery."

I agree with LaPan. I do wonder about the effect of intense fishing pressure on local pike populations. In other words, imagine (hypothetically) that ice fishermen take 200 pike out of a certain bay during January and February, and these pike are between 4 and 10 pounds. It's difficult to believe that this harvest won't limit the pike fishing in the areas around that bay during open-water months. Some fishing contests have instituted a minimum entry size, which is a step in the right direction.

Complicating matters is the fact that survival of winter-caught fish may be less than we think. Their reputations to the contrary, northerns are fairly fragile fish. As LaPan noted, their gills may freeze quickly in cold weather. But few anglers treat northerns gently. Most kick them back in the holes. So releasing fish, if not carefully, at least with hands instead of snowmobile boots would help.

A pike is owed that much.

# 2

# Beginnings

After two months of blizzards and ice floes, the North Country begins to stir, with a higher sun, longer afternoons, perhaps even a thaw or two. Like other wild creatures, pike respond to this change before we realize it is under way. They move up on the weed shelves, feed more aggressively. Late winter becomes a time of movement, of migration to spawning areas. The journey begins even as ice covers the water.

Pike spawn in the same area each year, drawn to their natal marsh by the familiar smell of decaying organic material on the bottom. Males arrive before females, but both sexes may stage for a month before spawning, which generally occurs when the water temperature reaches the mid-40s.

March represents a great turning of the country above the ice, too. The seamless white horizon groans in the convulsions of late winter. The earth emerges in fits and starts, laundered, scraped and pounded. This transitional period supposedly speaks of signs of spring, of looking ahead, but the bold little freshets of spring and haunting echoes of returning fowl have always made me feel the past.

Looking out over the graying ice of Lake Ontario, I could as well be looking at 12,000 B.C. when, give or take 1,000 years, humans first populated North America. I like to imagine casting spoons into a spring bay, a saber-toothed tiger prowling the shore, perhaps. Like spring anglers everywhere, I can count on being startled by the tail splash of a beaver, although this would be a *Whock!* to remember, as the adult giant beaver often reached a weight of 350 pounds.

Pike just seem to be the fish that belong in this picture. They not only look primeval, they are primeval. Evolutionary biologists emphasize how little their morphology has changed. As one report concludes, "The discovery of a paleocene pike in western Canada showed that the basic pike body form and feeding mechanism have persisted largely unchanged for at least 60 million years."

Some species of pike probably evolved from the herring-salmonid order of fish 80 million years ago. For years scientists believed that *Esox* got its start in northern Eurasia, evolving from *Palaeoesox fritschei* (60 million B.C.) through *Esox papyraceus* (30 million B.C.). According to this theory, the northern pike, as we know it, appeared some two million years ago in northern Europe and Asia. From there it spread to North America via the land bridge across the Bering Strait during the Ice Age.

In 1980, however, researchers discovered the fossilized skeleton *(Esox tiemani)* noted above in western Canada. The remains dated from at least 60 million years ago, and basically trashed the Asia-to-Alaska Ice Age theory of expansion.

Current theories have pike in North America *(Esox tiemani)* and Eurasia *(Palaeoesox fritschei)* evolving separately from the herring-salmonid order 80 million years ago. In Eurasia *Esox* developed into a warm-water species *(E. lepidotus)* that failed to survive the subsequent cold temperatures, leaving Europe and Asia without *Esox.* Meanwhile, the North American *Esox* evolved first into one species tolerant of warmer water, the muskellunge *(E. masquinongy)*, around 25 million B.C., and later a second species more tolerant of cold water—the northern pike *(E. lucius)*.

The northern pike then spread from North America to Asia and ultimately Europe during the Ice Age via that old land bridge in northeastern Asia. By the way, it's easier to understand the land bridge as vehicle for the dispersal of a species if you consider that it was some 400 miles wide and that pike are rapid colonizers. The thinking has pike spreading through marshy systems in this land mass and thereby reaching river systems in Asia. Sounds believable, I guess. But to tell the truth, I wouldn't get too invested in any particular evolutionary scheme.

In North America the natural pike distribution stretched from the sub-Arctic to the southern limits of the Great Lakes drainages. Pike came to inhabit waters of northern Asia, excluding desert and arid regions of China and central Asia and coastal areas, nearly reaching polar regions. In Europe pike distribution edged south to the northern edges of the Mediterranean region. In northern Europe pike eventually claimed many of the Scandinavian waters, save those in the mountainous areas of Norway. A freshwater fish almost exclusively, the pike would occupy one known salty habitat—the Baltic Sea.

The Baltic is also the site of the first known angling efforts. Specifically, anglers caught pike near the mouth of the Oder River in the Baltic Sea on spoons made of bronze and iron. As for sport fishing, the earliest mention comes from a 12th-century canon on the Marne, one Gui of Bazoches, who listed pike as a fish he enjoyed catching while visiting his uncle's home in the country.

Knowledge of the northern's feeding habits spread through Europe, and keepers used pike to control numbers of carp. In the 13th century, for instance, Count Thibault of Champagne stocked his pond with 3,520 carp, some 10,000 bream and roach, and six large pike. In the *Canterbury Tales* Chaucer writes of a person who has "many a . . . luce" in his pond—though it is unclear whether they're valued for food, sport, or crowd control.

Techniques for pike angling show up in the 14th century. A German text advised anglers to use a single strong hook baited with a minnow and a line covered with wire due to the pike's sharp teeth. Fifteenth-century Brits favored a bobber, a double hook, and a roach rubbed with camphor oil to make it shine and smell. That was the best bait from January through March—though worms worked then, too. Frogs were preferred bait in spring and fall.

The idea that pike provide their own unique sport followed. In the famed *Treatyse of Fysshynge wyth an Angle* came the 15th-century version of light tackle: "And yf ye lyst to haue a good sporte, thenne tye the corde [to which the hook baited with a frog or oiled minnow would be attached] to a gose fote [a goose's foot] and ye shall se god halynge [a good tug of war] whether the gose or the pyke shall haue the better." And you think the modern-day angler is gear-crazy.

## OVERSEAS

Mammoth pike persist in England and Ireland to this day, and perhaps because of this, the English have refined baitfishing into an art form. Though artificial lures are used frequently in Sweden, Finland, Demark, and France, natural baits—live and dead—continue to be more popular in Europe than here in North America. The English remain very serious about baiting big pike, and their live-bait rigs entail a complexity we would call exceptional. They begin by identifying those areas that hold the biggest fish, well aware that pike move with the seasons. They rely on dead baits in the discolored water of December, which they assume require pike to use their sense of smell to find food. They also use dead baits at various times during the early spring. In either case, anglers leave baits resting on bottom or insert a bit of plastic foam (or comparable material) inside the bait so that it floats just above the bottom.

The biggest pike, according to British pike authors John Bailey and Martyn Page, fall to paternostered baits. These are of two sorts. One is the fixed paternoster, a small boom off the main line that in effect holds the bait off the bottom. The other and more recent development involves a paternoster that allows the line to run freely. Hooking arrangements are also varied, but multiple-hooked rigs are standard. Running pike are struck quickly, and serious fishermen practice careful catch-and-release.

At times, when conditions dictate a searching presentation, the British rely on a roving bait—that is, a live baitfish towing a bob, sometimes fixed with a tiny sail on top of the float. British pike angler Mick Brown notes that distances of 150 yards can be achieved with this approach, particularly if the line is greased to keep it afloat and the bobber's progress can be followed through binoculars. These guys may like to see that bobber dive, but they're no barefoot boys dangling worms beneath corks.

Whereas the variety in American fishing comes from countless types of artificials, the variety in British (and Irish) pike fishing appears in the range of natural baits. Occasionally, these are colored or preserved (particularly smelt or herring). Roach, herring, perch, and in particular (artificially reared) trout serve as the preferred live or dead bait. The hatchery trout, according to British writers Bailey and Page, "are born to be killed [so that] the natural-born fish of our waters are left unmolested. Pike men in these later years of this century must be conservationists to a great extent, and the roach and dace stocks of our rivers especially are alarmingly depleted in many lowland areas."

Like their American counterparts, British anglers worry about the problems that develop when pike and trout share water—though their concerns don't necessarily proceed along the same path. Many of the biggest pike come from trout waters, which disturbs the purists. Pike purists, that is. As Bailey and Page note, "To them [purists] a pike that has waxed fat in a put-and-take trout fishery is not as 'genuine' as, say a wild, lean Scottish fish." Bailey and Page, for their part, see matters differently: "Generally, trout-water pike have never been caught before and this gives them a tremendous, glowing freshness and in my own view, it is hard to imagine a prettier pike than an immaculate mid-twenty that has been feeding on rainbows."

Those are the sentiments of pike anglers, of course, and in truth trout anglers in Europe are no happier about pike in their pools than are their American counterparts—particularly if the streams in question hold wild fish. In that case, pike are dispatched by whatever means necessary. Mick Brown writes about an invitation to fish a trout lake for the purpose of thinning the pike population. Finding them was easy. Prior to stocking, the trout were kept in cages, attached to docks. Guess where the pike were?

In short, the British consider pike fishing a chess match. Some of the biggest pike have been caught many times, which only seems to increase their stature, leaving them esteemed old specimens that require consummate skill and total commitment. Some anglers fish from boats; some troll spoons and spinners. Spinnerbaits are becoming more popular, as are artificials in general. But live baits remain the backbone of the fishery in Britain—not, as one writer observes, because they are fun to fish (he admits they aren't), but rather because the true trophy fisherman sees artificials as "Mickey Mouse."

## LIVE BAIT IN NORTH AMERICA

Fishing in North America took a different turn. Alexis de Toqueville and other foreign observers noted a feverish mobility and industry in 19th-century American culture, and it's reasonable to assume that active comportment influenced the development of fishing strategies, too. Angling accounts and catalogs from back then include numerous references to minnow rigs, harnesses, and such, reflecting the American marriage of bait and movement.

Rigged with various harnesses and contraptions, minnows were likely to stay hooked even when flung and dragged about. Anglers drifted in boats, with live bait hung beneath bobbers, but trolling became the most popular pike presentation. Getting a minnow to a fish was no small matter in the century before spinning reels.

Shiners, chubs, and suckers catch northerns today, just as they did 100 years ago. Bait is particularly valuable during the pre-spawn, when the biggest pike in the lake move into the shallowest water. You'll often read fantastic magazine articles about the great pike fishing at this time, but in my experience catching them is not as easy as writers would have you think. For one thing, pike move constantly during the spring. Finding them, moreover, offers no guarantee, since their mood can complicate matters. I suppose you could call these fish lethargic but hungry—lethargic because the water temperature remains in the 30s, hungry because the upcoming spawn requires energy.

The result is a window of fishing in 3 to 10 feet of water outside spawning swamps. Some anglers, for the record, report success with Floating Rapalas fished very slowly near cover. I have caught neither pre-spawn nor (immediately) post-spawn pike in this fashion. I've done better fly fishing, but in the end bait probably gives you the best chance. As noted above, the British fish dead bait at this time of year, often on a quick-strike rig. Pike may actually feed on yet-to-decompose baitfish and panfish. Why not? The food is there, and it can be scooped up with little trouble. In fact, we usually catch at least one northern every year during our annual bullhead weekend in April. The oddity is not only that the fish take a nightcrawler but also that

***Pre-spawn fish are sluggish, but may respond to dead bait fished near the bottom in a technique borrowed from the Brits.***

they strike in turbid water during the middle of the night—none of which could be classified as typical pike behavior. Perhaps these fish really are sniffing around for food, or maybe they're just picking up some bad habits from hanging around with bullheads.

After the spawn, living, swimming bait becomes a top choice. The standard live-bait operation, regardless of time of year, begins with 10- to 20-pound-test line, depending on the size of the snags in your lake and of the pike you're after. Select bait in the 4- to 8-inch range. Suckers, creek chubs, and golden shiners are probably the most popular choices, and they should be hooked lightly through the back (through the lips without a bobber) with a single size 1/0 hook snelled on a wire leader. As noted above, quick-strike hook harnesses are quite effective, should you choose them. A single split shot keeps the bait at a predetermined depth. Adjust the bobber so that the bait swims a foot or so above the weeds. Avoid "pike-sized" bobbers. Instead choose a small float that offers little resistance once it plunges below the surface and the pike begins a run.

My friend Ron Kolodziej is a guide on New York's Sacandaga Reservoir, site of the 46-pound, 2-ounce North American record pike, and he fishes this way during the post-spawn of early May. His biggest pike in the spring of 1999 was an 18½-pounder, which doesn't seem that big until you consider that he is fishing for pike on purpose and doing so four hours from New York City. Some spring mornings he gets four or five fish over 10 pounds fishing in this fashion.

Kolodziej drifts slowly through the shallows or positions his boat outside spawning areas on shallow shoals not far from deep water, his thinking being that the biggest fish like nothing better than a short commute to the hunting ground. He tosses out a couple of suckers, and makes an afternoon of it. It reminds me of the stories I've heard of hunting tigers with a tethered cow.

The British might put sails on their floats, but Americans sometimes go crazy and row or paddle in and out of structure, towing the bobber and minnow some 30 to 50 feet behind the boat. Hook the minnow through the lips if this is your strategy.

The thrill comes once the "sting" begins. The bobber bounces around for a moment. A nervous minnow gets everybody's attention. Sometimes it means nothing. Other times you look away, look back, and your bobber is gone. As with tip-ups during the winter, the fish will run before turning the bait around and swallowing it. With a quick-strike rig, of course, the angler sets the hook immediately; a traditional single hook requires a brief wait.

Fishing with a float is only one of the ways to present live minnows. Still-fishing on the bottom can sometimes interest sluggish post-spawn pike that won't bother with an active suspended bait. This bottom-fishing technique can be quite effective so long as the bottom remains relatively free of hang-ups—which is often the case in early spring. Don't expect pike to slam the minnow, either. More likely you'll feel a couple of slow tugs before the pike moves off with the bait.

You can cover more area by slowly dragging a minnow on a jighead or spinner-jig. The latter rig can be particularly effective when you work it along the lip of a cove or off either side of a point. Try bouncing it down a gradual incline in the bottom. A pike may be reluctant to chase down artificials, but it might just muster up the strength to gobble down a succulent dead chub with a cute little twinkle above its head.

## SEINING YOUR OWN

As a young angler, I was fascinated with live-bait fishing for northerns. Part of my interest involved the drama of predation, which is what appealed to me about hawks and owls carrying living, struggling creatures back to their nests. Live-bait fishing let me participate in that dynamic in a palpable way by feeding one live thing to another,

*Sluggish or not, early-spring pike remain the ultimate boatside battlers. Note bobber, which has slipped a bit in the fray.*

which I must admit doesn't thrill me like it once did. I hear this growth is a sign of mental health.

I loved getting bait, too, if for no other reason than that it was the first step to catching pike, a fish so big that the bait had to be netted or trapped. Such was the situation one summer during my annual two-week visit to my great-aunt and -uncle's home in the Adirondacks. Usually Uncle Frank, who was nearing 70 at the time, and I went shore fishing, for we had no boat. But he knew how much I wanted to catch a pike, and so he arranged a trip for us with his landlord, who kept his boat on nearby Lake Champlain. My uncle was retired, so it was our chore to get the bait in the afternoon.

We parked beside a beaver pond, and Uncle Frank walked around the car, opened the trunk, and removed a wire-mesh, cylinder-shaped cage with a length of clothesline attached. He unclipped the little cage so that it fell apart into two symmetrical halves. My uncle, who delighted in such magician moves, withdrew a couple of pieces of bread crust from a paper bag and placed them in the trap. "This is a min-

*Note four-foot distance between small bobber and shiner, designed for fishing along a six-foot drop-off in May.*

now trap," he explained. He was a kind man, a gentleman who wore a tie every day of his life—whether going to church or taking me fishing. Even at age seven I was aware of how much he enjoyed the simple efficiency of this tool. He saved everything in his garage, and I wouldn't be surprised if he'd been saving this minnow trap some 30 years for just this moment.

He looked around on the side of the dirt road. "We need some weight," he said, stooping to pick up a baseball-sized rock. He dropped it in one of the halves of the wire cage and clipped them together. Then he tossed the trap out into the water and looped the clothesline around one of the beaver spikes poking out of the shoreline mud.

After a few minutes, he rapped the dead tobacco from his pipe and announced that it was time to check the operation. I grabbed the rope and hustled the trap from the water. A fat, silvery green and black ball of chubs batted against the mesh, like baseball cards against bike spokes. My uncle unclipped the trap and dumped the creek chubs into the bait bucket. "There's about two dozen good ones. These beaver-pond chubs are great bait, fat and lively," he said. "They'll do the trick."

That evening I maintained surveillance on the minnow bucket all the way to the fishing spot, and I had one chub all picked out—a robust 5-incher. I hooked it through the back and over the side of the boat went the whole rig. I watched the bobber, watched it, looked away, and delighted in the electricity of trying to relocate it when I returned my attention to fishing. There it was, placidly drifting. I checked the bait—still wiggling. Back down. We must have been practically under the Champlain Bridge, because I remember looking up and seeing cars far overhead. At one point I looked back for my bobber, but it wasn't in sight. I was small and absolutely stuffed inside my life jacket, and I had to get to my feet to see over the sides of the boat. Gone. It truly was gone.

I reeled up, and when the line came tight, I felt a tug. Then more tugs, strong ones. I had a fish.

I jammed the rod butt in my life jacket and held on with my right hand and reeled with my left. It was the early days of spinning, and my reel had little if any drag, and even less give. Suddenly a great northern pike came flying out of the water, sprayed the boat, then dove beneath it.

There was my uncle with the net. "Okay, take your time," he said, "and pull up easily." I did, and he slipped the net beneath the pike and swung it into the boat, where it beat a tattoo on the bottom. I just stared at that fish. "Well, yessir," he said. "You did a fine job. First rate."

Later the pike proved too big for the kitchen sink, curling around one of the sides. My uncle measured it on the back porch, and his rule read 24 inches, but we

*Try to place bobber and shiner near shoreline weeds early in the season.*

called it 25. "Let's see what he's been eating," my uncle said. And there in the stomach was a half-eaten panfish and one fat, partially skinned, 5-inch chub.

Uncle Frank had a stroke a couple of years after that and couldn't fish any more.
But I remember all of what he taught me, particularly the idea that good bait equals
good fishing. For northerns, in particular, it became a sort of code—regardless of
where I fished. At Cedar Point on the St. Lawrence River, where I spent my summers
in the years after that first northern, the word on pike was simple: sucker minnows in
weedy water. That's how Don Wolf, the park caretaker and fishing and hunting guru,
caught them in fall while he was repairing the docks. That's how Red Williams and
other campers caught them in May before bass season opened. My cousin Mike and I

used to fish pike in these waters, too, and while we didn't catch that many northerns, we had an absolute riot getting the bait.

We were 10 or 11 at the time, and we'd seine the creek that ran through his family's farm. Sometimes Mike's older brother, Don, would join us. We learned to work in the current, one of us on each side of the creek. Then one of us would cross at a shallow spot and we'd both slosh to shore, sweeping the seine quickly so the bait couldn't escape. We'd flop the net on the bank. Unfolded, the wet mesh would reveal a twitching ball of crabs, dragonfly nymphs, polliwogs, shiners, sunfish, rock bass, mud, and leeches, along with the occasional adder and water snake.

We'd pluck out the crabs and shiners and pop them in the bucket. Bass bait. Then we'd slog downstream to where the creek slipped beneath some meadow banks and ran a little deeper. The dark holes held sucker minnows and creek chubs, and we'd pull through a deep pool, fighting and laughing over who had the steep side, and come up with a net full of suckers, creek chubs, perch, juvenile largemouth bass, and often as not a small northern or two—the same size as the other fish. We'd release the baby pike and bass, but not the suckers. They'd bump and bang into the thin tin sides of the bait bucket. And, we'd listen to them, convinced that we were but hours away from landing the biggest northern in the St. Lawrence River.

*Seining your own.*

# 3

# Bad Guys

For those of us living in the North Country, March can seem interminable, the month as Pat McManus puts it, that God made in case eternity proves too short. Infinity aside, April suns eventually warm the shallow, dark-bottomed bays, pike spawn, and whatever feeding activity there has been in the pre-spawn shuts down for a couple of weeks.

Pike spawn in shallow protected areas and flooded backwaters, usually in 3 to 6 feet of water over sandy or silty bottoms with decaying vegetation. If these areas become unavailable, pike will spawn in deeper, colder water, though such spots represent a nuptial bed of last resort. More productive spawning occurs inshore. Researchers report finding eggs attached to reeds, timber, even flooded meadow grass. Studies conducted at Lake George in Minnesota and Conesus Lake in New York both found that "pike spawning never occurred in cattail areas, but that all other vegetation were used. . . . Pike tended to avoid heavy and thick types of vegetation (cattail, buttonbrush, brush)." Researchers studying Oneida Lake in New York found that "pike eggs were distributed throughout the marsh where the bottom had been covered with vegetation and flooded to a depth of 25 cm or more."

Males and females can become sexually mature after one year, though two to four years is more typical. Males prefer bigger females. Upon the approach of a male, an unripe female assumes a threatening posture or tosses her head to throw him off. A ripe female shows acceptance of the male by swimming slowly forward. The two pike line up eye to eye so that their sexual organs are in alignment. The pair slows and the male moves into position and, with a flip of his tail, mixes the extruding sperm with extruding eggs.

Pike perform these brief mating acts repeatedly for a period of some three hours or more. Warming water cranks up the activity. In one study, three males and one female copulated on the average of once every five minutes; in another, one female and three small males were observed spawning for three consecutive days. There's no evidence of territoriality, and a dense aggregation of spawners often gathers. Mating, in the words of one researcher, is both "polygamous and promiscuous."

Preoccupied and in shallow water, spawning northerns remain quite vulnerable to human predation. Archaeological middens show pike to have been among the Indians' favorite species. Pike were unavailable to most colonial anglers, however, since their original distribution included sub-Arctic Canada and the Great Lakes drainage but ended in Lake Champlain in present-day western Vermont. On the Atlantic seaboard, from Maine to Virginia (the center of colonial America), *Esox* meant pickerel. Even at the start pike inhabited the American imagination as a northern exotic of the great interior wilderness.

Colonists traveled to the interior, of course, but the fishing they did on those excursions must have been limited. It's not like you'd reach a campsite and say, "Hey, Nathaniel, do me a favor and keep an eye out for any suspicious-looking Indians or trappers. I'm going down to the creek edge to make a few casts with my Jitterbug."

The earliest encounters, given colonial settlement patterns and the pike's range in North America, probably occurred on the banks of one of the lakes or rivers in the Great Lakes system, perhaps during spawning. Even today, you can see big fish slowly moving through the shallows of these waters, indifferent to all offerings. These fish must have proved quite tempting to early colonists who, by all indications, were quite familiar with the "long fork."

Nothing new here, however. The earliest record of human interactions with pike come from prehistoric dwelling sites, where pike were consumed as food along with other fish. Of particular note is the discovery of pike bones on the Yorkshire coast of England. The site dates from the post-Pleistocene, pre-Roman period around 5,000 B.C. and reveals the presence of harpoon heads near the fish bones at an old peat bog. Could it be that the locals were doing a bit of pike spearing during spawning time?

French Creek finds its source in the first ribbon of hardwood ridges just inland from the New York side of the St. Lawrence River. It begins as a clear-water creek, with clay tribs increasing and clouding its flow and eventually creating French Creek flats. In spring this marshy complex hosts spawning fish of all sorts. Pickerel, pike, bullheads, smallmouth and largemouth bass, perch and other panfish, suckers, dogfish, even occasional muskies frequent French Creek. Northerns are among the first visitors, and in some years begin spawning as early as the first week in April.

My mother's side of the family has farmed the land along French Creek for close to a century, my grandparents coming over from southern France as part of the great European migration. After that, their sons farmed here; now it's done by a grandson—my cousin Don—and a great-grandson, Don's son, Jeff. It was a tributary to the main creek that provided us with such great sport in early bait-collecting adventures. We also used to fish here for bullheads and panfish and, later, in the evening, prowl its shores looking for bigger fish to spear.

A bridge divided the upper and lower creeks. Below the bridge, 10-foot-wide riffles wound through pasture. Here we speared suckers, milky shapes that shifted in the lemon glow of the flashlight. Above the bridge, the creek had no channel and was wider and shallower, flooding into an open meadow in the high water of spring. That was where pike spawned.

And here was where my cousin Mike and I headed one cool April evening many years ago. The dates on pictures from that weekend say it occurred in 1960, which made me nine, him eight. Mike's brother Don had speared an 8-pounder there the night before, and we were out the door just ahead of shouts of, "Don't go spearing each other!" We headed down the tarred road some several hundred yards to the bridge dividing the upper grassy flats from the lower creek. The yellow lights of sucker spearers perforated the blackness below the bridge. We went the opposite way, upstream into flooded meadow grass.

Mike owned the hip boots, so he got to spear first. I wore rubber pac books and was designated flashlight holder. After one try, we'd switch flashlight for spear, pacs for hippers. We sneaked along the shore, Mike easing through the shallow grasses, behind and below me by a step. I kept the beam some 5 feet out from the shore so that it illuminated his line of fire. The clear amber shallows showed a lively underwater world—a flash of perch here, another small shadow there. Then a flat head, a big flat head, and broad back. A dogfish turned in the light. Mike lunged at the fish, jamming the spear deep into the muck behind the tail.

"Why that duckass," Mike said. He took the flashlight from me and scanned the weeds next to shore, hoping to spot the fish.

"My turn," I said, grabbing the spear. I sat down on the damp meadow and started to pull off my pacs. "Let me see those hip boots."

"Just a minute. Hold it," he said, lowering the light. "There's a pike right out there." At first I didn't believe him, but there was something in the way he slowly returned the light to the water that got my attention. There it was, just 5 feet out from shore next to a reed bed: eyes, and a long shape just above the grass.

Mike clicked off the light. "Get ready to nail him, 'cause he's moving next time this light hits the water. Aim for the eyes."

I picked up the spear and edged toward the water. I could make out the sketchy outline of the reed copse, next to which was the pike. I reared back.

"Now!" Mike said, clicking on the light. Spots, fins, eyes. The eyes!

I jabbed the spear down, digging the tines into the mud. I felt a wiggle, a glorious wiggle on the end of my spear, and saw the waves continue even as I held the shaft. I tossed the thrashing fish back in the meadow grass, where it flopped with wet smacks. In the light it looked huge. From photos, I'd say 5, maybe 6 pounds.

Then we heard a car on the road, the first of the evening. It stopped on the bridge. Game protector.

We were stuck. We could see the glow of the farmhouse on the hill, but we couldn't go back across the bridge with the pike. Walking upstream above the weedy flat would mean a 4-mile hike through the woods—and we'd still get wet crossing the creek.

"We've got to cut across right here," Mike said. "It's not that deep."

"Not that deep" has long been the standard measure of shallow water, though as most North Country folks know, it is subject to seasonal variations, which was the case now. We hit waist-deep about 10 yards offshore, but it never got deeper than that all the way across, which was a good thing because we were afraid to shine the light.

"Hey, you kids, what are you doing?" boomed off the bridge. We hit high gear with that and didn't slow down till we reached the safety of the farmhouse kitchen. There we learned that the game protector was Donny's idea of a practical joke, but Mike and I didn't care. We'd gotten a pike, a big one, and it was time to tell the tale of the hunt.


## EARLY NOTIONS OF NORTHERNS

As I recall, the adults sitting around the table were concerned mostly about pike slime on the linoleum and what we'd put on for dry clothes. There was little concern for the fish hanging from the end of the spear; if anything, they shared in our success.

Then, as now, northerns had their benefactors and detractors, a tradition in place long before the great pike-spearing adventure, before even the European invasion of North America. In that respect, pike are closer to trout and salmon than to the bass, the latter being limited to the American stage. The salmonids and pike already had their reputations; that much the Europeans brought with them.

Pike inhabited waters north of the early literate civilizations of the Mediterranean Sea. The first written reference comes from a fourth-century Roman poet, one Decimus Magnus Ausonius, who'd ventured east to tutor a future Germanic emperor and recorded his impressions of the Rhine River and its inhabitants in the poem "Mosella." Professor Richard Hoffman translates it from Latin:

*A dweller in backwaters does enjoy a proper Latin name.*
*Lucius besieges the complaining frogs*
*in obscure holes among sedges and mud.*
*His meat is not for the dining table*
*but sold at cheap shops smoky with its reeking stink.*

Here in its first media appearance the pike gets saddled with the label of "backwater ambusher," with flesh unfit for proper people. An animal's status often begins with how good it is to eat. Humans are predators, after all. It stands to reason that value as food would be an initial consideration. And pike? They are complete ambiguity, with delectable flesh and a good deal of it, but bones in odd places make it difficult to prepare.

The poem also outlines the rudiments of the pike's "bad" behavior. Contemporary writers and editors may think themselves clever when they characterize pike as "wolves," "water wolves," or, as I once read, "water wolves of the weed beds," but in fact they're about 1,500 years late on their metaphors. Then, as now, the pike's appearance left a haunting impression: a wolf's face, duck-billed jaws, and a snaky, slimy body. People in the Middle Ages saw little chance in these physical assignations. They marked the fish as special—a creature to be both feared and revered.

Legend has it that in 526 Theodoric, ruler of the Ostrogoths, died in fright at the dinner table when he looked at the markings on a pike's head and saw the face of an enemy he'd just executed. Others found religious symbolism in the markings on the pike's head, specifically the tools of Christ's crucifixion: cross, ladder, hammer, nails, thorns, whip, and sponge—all the result of Christ carrying his cross through a brook in which the pike lived. Some saw more sinister messages in the markings, claiming the pike to be the purveyor of harmful deeds, created by the devil to vex God. The pike became the "aquatic wolf . . . the tyrant of the waters." The pike's predation on smaller fish served as an allegory for the ways enemies of the church preyed upon the assemblage.

Its demonic spirit notwithstanding, the pike commanded respect, an equally important characteristic of its cultural and social construction. Stories have it eating fishermen, becoming king of the fishes. The pike came to signify achievement. The knight who won a great tournament held in France in 1177 received a large pike for his efforts.

Pike eventually evoked commercial interest, receiving mention in contracts and disputes and even serving as gifts among the nobility. Archaeological excavations reveal ample evidence of pike, second only to zander (a European version of walleye). In early fish stores in France pike cost four times more than carp. The pike's white, flaky flesh was (and is) a common ingredient in gefilte fish, a traditional Jewish dish. In short, pike became popular table fare, sign from God or not.

In 1558 pike made their first appearance in a biological text, thanks to the work of Conrad Gesner. Readers expecting a clinical approach to pike might be disappointed. Gesner's pike grab mules by the lips, eat dogs, and chomp down on the feet of peasant girls. Gesner included angling strategies, food value, even the use of pike for medicinal purposes, claiming that pike ashes serve as an antidote for pain in shameful places. And they say North American Indians never left anything to waste.

In the 1577 publication *The Arte of Angling* William Samuels notes that pike have no fear of man, and makes recommendations for angling. Samuels also confirms the existence of a 267-year-old pike, beginning the combination of how-to advice and mythical tales that dominates the sporting pages to this very day.

Izaak Walton has quite a bit to say about pike, too, calling the fish a "tyrant," the salmon a king. Walton's attitude about pike reflects the English gentry's disposition. As fly-fishing historian David Ledlie has noted, the effect of British sentiments cannot be overstated when looking at the formation of American attitudes on the subject.

## PIKE IN AMERICA

In his book *Northern Pike Fishing* Kit Bergh observes that "the North American Indians seemed in general much more aware of the significance of pike, with tribes named for them." But invading Europeans brought a different view, one lifted from Walton's template constructed in moats and chalk streams, one that held all fish to be poor cousins (at best) to trout and salmon. Some fish (read: pike) were downright bad fellows.

Consider the following account written by Genio Scott in the 1869 text *Fishing in American Waters:* "It [the pike] preys on any living thing from a duckling to a swallow, and from a mouse to a frog. Everything is game to this wolf of the pond that moves at night, hides in the watery sedges, sneaks upon his prey and devastates and terrorizes the world of the inland seas."

Nevertheless, Scott thoroughly enjoyed the thrill of fishing for pike. Other anglers apparently did, too, fishing them with frogs and minnows, often in conjunction with artificial lures. The Spinning Minnow was considered a hot "lure" in the mid–19th century. The head or front portion remained stationary, while the rear part (with the minnow sewn on) spun. McCarg's and Buel's spoons, made of nickel with protruding red and/or white feathers, remained popular choices, too. These could well have been the first American lures designed specifically for northern pike. They were often "skittered," or pulled through the water with a cane pole, whereas the Spinning Minnow was usually trolled or drifted. Catalogs of the day began touting pike-sized hooks and minnow rigs, and pike-sized spinners and spoons.

"Sports" (like Scott) may have been more kindly disposed to northerns than were their guides or those who lived close to pike. The northerns gave a wild, thrilling account of themselves close to the boat, which must have been exhilarating to the city anglers. Pike fillets, moreover, are delicious when fried in cast-iron skillet over a shoreline fire. The guides were the ones doing the cleaning and cooking, however, and compared with trout and bass, pike were slimy, skinny, difficult to handle and dress, and filled with Y-bones. More trouble than they were worth, particularly next to brookies, bass, and glass-eyed pike (as walleyes were called). If the sports liked to catch pike, well, that's why they were called "sports."

The pike was a predator, and as the 19th century ended, few thinking men entertained the idea of a predator having redeeming qualities. Such a contention would

*Pike can make you pay. Stan Warner.*

have been preposterous. There were bounties not only on coyotes and wolves, but on bears and eagles, too. Dispatching predators—be they furred, finned, or feathered—was nothing more or less than a civic duty.

This was a time when appearances mattered, when fish were anthropomorphised to better understand their character. And pike looked like outlaws, with underslung criminal-like jaws, vacant yellow eyes, and needle-sharp teeth. A thick, smelly mucus coated their serpentine bodies. They were vicious, bloodthirsty, sneaky. And if that weren't enough, pike actually behaved and acted the way their stereotype suggested, lurking in weedy backwaters, ready to fall upon unsuspecting travelers. An angler would be reeling in a smallmouth or walleye and a pike would ambush the hapless fish, rip it off the hook, and gobble it down. They might as well have been foxes snatching chickens from henhouses.

To an extent, sentiment varied by region. As Scott notes, "It is an interesting fact that the pike is abhorred in certain waters. When you are fishing for salmon in the Wye as an example, or for muscallunge in the St. Lawrence. . . . If it so happens that there is nothing else to catch, the pike becomes at once a game fish." Other anglers caught them while fishing for bass, walleyes, and muskies, and from turn-of-the-century accounts they were not all that happy about it. In trout country folks were even less kindly disposed to pike.

I have a particular memory from long ago of visiting my Aunt Margaret and Uncle Frank's home in the Adirondacks one Easter. I remember going for a ride with my dad and uncle along Lake Champlain. We saw hunters walking along a railroad bed that followed the contour of a brushy marsh south of Port Henry. My dad knew the men, and he pulled the car off the road so we could watch them shoot a pike, which was not only legal but quite popular.

"There. Ed sees one," my dad said, pointing to one of the hunters, a red-plaid old-timer some 50 yards away. We watched him raise his rifle. *Karong!* The shot sound echoed off the railbed, across the swamp.

"Got 'im!" Ed yelled to his friend, who stood farther down the tracks.

We got out and walked over. Ed and his partner wore hunting boots, and had no intention of retrieving the fish. They talked with my dad and uncle, and then continued on along the railbed in search of more pike. They may as well have been shooting rats at the dump.

And that made perfect sense, especially given the way pike were blamed for the demise of the brook trout. We now know that the real villains were paved roads and resulting fishing pressure, along with a long-term habitat deterioration that permitted the entrance of yellow perch to the waterways. But such gradual changes escaped the notice of anglers of the era.

The role of dangerous predator also explains part of the pike's curious appeal, too. After all, in order for a predator to be dangerous, it must possess some quality to an extraordinary degree—as in smart as a fox, eyes like a hawk, and so forth. With northerns, it was the speed and suddenness of their attack. Here is our 19th-century pike angler Genio Scott:

*By blue lake marge, upon whose breast*
*The water lilies love to rest,*
*Lurking beneath those leaves of green*
*The fierce pike seeks his covert screen,*
*And thence with sudden plunge and leap,*
*Swift as a shaft through air may sweep,*
*He seizes, rends, and bears away*
*To hidden lair his struggling prey.*

The pitiful plight of the prey certainly adds a nice touch. And who wouldn't want to battle a predator that, in the words of D. H. Lawrence, could make the "small fish fly like splinters"?

By the first decade or so of the 20th century, certain grudging declarations of the worth of pike begin to appear. Dixie Carroll, an important sportswriter of the day, has the following to say in a *National Sportsman* article:

For downright cussedness, old man, you got to tack the blue-ribbon on the pike. This vicious old wolf of the weed-beds and rushes, known by a dozen other names and particularly named as pickerel by a big bunch of the knights of the rod and reel, is about the meanest all-round fin in the whole society of the watery recesses. . . . That final scrap, when he kicks water in your face and leers at you with his mean-looking eyes before he makes a straight-away run for about 40 or 50 feet, as you push on the thumb pressure, is bound to be a lively few minutes, and when you finally slip him the gaff you can feel sort of lucky. In fact, a pike is never really landed until you have him sizzling in the spider for the evening chuck.

Other fish might bring satisfaction or success to an outdoor excursion, but pike brought the excitement. They looked bigger than they were. They crashed the party. Ate the other fish. Bit the lines, shattered the rods. They struck with a rush, ended with a flurry; in short, they slammed some adventure into every fishing trip. Pike were truly different from other fish, even other members of *Esox* family—larger than pickerel, more sudden than muskies. They were "sauvages," wilder than their British counterparts. In a sense, they weren't pike at all. They were Great Northerns!

## TWENTIETH-CENTURY TRADITIONS

Stories and articles about pike do appear in these years, but their sum hardly represents a body of literature. As an experiment, I reviewed every issue of *Field & Stream* between 1931 and 1951 and found only four articles on pike. Certain issues contained four or five articles on bass. And it wasn't like the editors were dodging esoteric topics: I even found several articles on fly fishing for walleyes. Of the four pike articles, only one explained how to catch a pike. Another described a new method for cleaning them in which the author scalded the scales from the pike. (Accompanying photos showed how to do it!) A third article was about a big pike adventure. The fourth was a photo essay, so to speak, which exposed evidence (literally) of pike predation on ducklings by picturing an eviscerated 21-inch pike on a newspaper, alongside the three ducklings taken from its stomach.

Remarkably, during this same period northern pike appeared on a number of different covers—breaking rods, tearing through nets, eating ducklings, chasing canoeists. Okay, I'm kidding about the last one, but not the first three. It is as if pike would be missed if they weren't there, as if people found the presence of pike exciting, enjoyed the unpredictable element they injected into a Saturday fishing trip. As wilderness fish, it is not surprising that we came to look to them for a little wildness in our day-to-day fishing lives—particularly as the rest of our existence became increasingly citified.

But it's not like you had to fish for them on purpose—and therefore the absence of angling advice. The prevailing sentiment of pike-as-afterthought shows up quite clearly in lure advertisements. Pikie Minnows were touted as bass and muskie lures, with pike sometimes mentioned in the smaller print. Dardevle ads showed an angler with a string of bass. The bold print exclaimed: BASS! MUSKIES!! WALLEYES!!!

By the 1950s some explicit pike ads began to appear. Lou Eppinger conceded what everyone else knew about red and white spoons, and Dardevle advertisements began to include pictures of big northern pike. Red-eye Wigglers and Paul Bunyan spoons (which were more or less the same lure pattern) followed suit.

There was no selling of strategy, as with lure advertisements for other species. Any pike lures played to the pike's bloodthirsty reputation—literally—as can be seen in one bleeding minnow advertisement (in which a "blood" tablet was inserted in the

*It's all about the teeth, as this toothy grin reveals. Note Red Eye Wiggler, still an effective pike lure today. Lee Ellsworth.*

side of the lure). Interestingly, the advertisement pictured a generic pike-muskie and didn't mention "pike" in the print. My favorite was the Cree-Duck, an imitation duckling with a spinner on the tail to imitate paddling feet. The ad pictured an Indian guide straining while he held a pair of huge pike. Some strategy, those imitation ducklings. Perhaps 100 years from now an angling historian will come along and argue that the "Cree-Duck" was a pike permutation of Schweibert's *Matching the Hatch*, which so enthralled the mid-1950s trout-fishing community.

Charles Waterman, Paul Schullery, and others have noted the danger of assuming that angling in print equals angling astream. Some anglers certainly did fish seriously for pike, but the point becomes clouded by the fact that anglers in mid-20th-century America tended to involve themselves in a variety of seasonal pursuits. In contrast, to-day's anglers are more likely to pursue one species through the various seasons. In broad terms, there is little evidence to suggest that pike fishing was an operation to be taken seriously, like trout fishing. No one worried about a secret pike hole, at least no one I ever met. Fishing for them remained a casual affair. As a kid, that's how I rather impatiently experienced my elders' response to northerns.

I remember fishing with Uncle Frank in the Adirondack Mountains. He hooked a northern on a plug and reared back, as if to encourage the fish to jump. It tail-walked right across in front of me on shore, splashing water and throwing the plug. My uncle, the master of understatement, reeled in his plug and examined it. He winked at me, the way he did when he did when he was about to trump my ace in pinochle.

It was the ultimate casual statement, a maneuver he never would have chanced with a trout. But pike were different. It was hard to take fishing for them seriously when two months earlier men had been shooting them from the same shoreline. On a more practical level a trout had an actual food value, unmatched by a bony pike. And so Uncle Frank's casual approach. Make them jump, get the most of the playing. What better way to accommodate their ambiguous role in the American fishing scene at midcentury?

As in ancient European myth and legend, pike in North America came to be both revered and feared, valued and trashed. We want them around so they can remind us of what no longer is. Northerns have definitely benefited from a cooling of the passion for killing varmints. More and more anglers seem to appreciate fishing for them these days. But the pike's reputation as a shady character lingers on, like patches of spring snow in the North Woods.

*There is much to admire about pike.*

# 4

# Life and Death
# in a Weedbed

There is a time in April when you can smell the upturned earth, when the countryside glows pale-frog green, when it is warm enough to fish bullheads at night. Liquid mornings hold the promise not only of fine days, but of full seasons as well. The shallows of pike lakes warm, with temperatures climbing into the upper 40s. It would make for pleasant copy to claim this as the time to fish for pike, but in fact it is not. Finished with spawning, pike will begin feeding soon, but not before they've had some rest.

Naturally, this post-spawn period varies with location: June in northern Canada, May in southern Canada, mid- to late April in the northern United States. Whatever the location, pike more or less bask in the receding floods. Too spent to chase food, they may hold in cover, hang along creek bottoms, or move slowly towards more open bays. You can sometimes see them ghosting through the shallows, neither perturbed by your presence nor particularly interested in a bait or a lure.

They are in a zone. If they had cigarettes, they'd smoke them. Their reproductive tasks are complete. Their progeny swim.

## BABY TEETH

Life begins in a flooded edge or field as a fertilized egg, 2 millimeters in diameter, that falls to the bottom as part of a small cluster. Development depends on water temperatures of 50 degrees and sufficient dissolved oxygen. Light also stimulates hatching, which occurs at a relatively early developmental stage.

Newly hatched larvae swim upward, attach to vegetation, and live off their embryonic sacs. Mucus secretion allows the pike to hang vertically from leaves and stalks, beginning a lifelong dependence on slime and on camouflage, the stripes, in the words of one researcher, serving as "adaptations to clinging to vegetation in spawning shallows."

Little pike remain attached for two or three days, depending on the water temperature, but continue to grow. First the finfold divides, then pectoral fins develop, finally the mouth and gills open. Over the next few days their pectoral fins vibrate, and they begin breathing through gills. The swim bladder fills with air, the adhesive glands shrink, and they begin swimming.

Soon they snap at food particles. Their wedge-shaped heads become pikelike, their eyes mobile, their vision binocular. They feed furiously on midges and tiny crustacea. The head, jaws, eyes, and tail develop more rapidly than the body. At 2 inches the fins and scales emerge distinctly, as the fish make increasing use of inshore vegetative zones and begin feeding on the larvae of other fish. Before that point, the lateral line plays a relatively minimal role in hunting and is used mostly for detecting danger. After little pike reach the 2-inch mark, the lateral line comes more into play and permits them to enter weeded areas at low light for hunting.

The primary stimulus for feeding is visual, however. Typically, a little pike waits for food, but begins searching when a meal fails to show up. It will "mark down" a prey, stalking carefully, keeping its eyes on the target, correcting its body direction like we might line up a pool shot. The pike then forms an S-shape and snaps straight, propelling itself toward the prey. If the mark is true, the little pike sucks in as it snaps. Success is about 30 percent initially, though that increases with practice. Three days after changing to external food, the little pike nearly always hit their target, taking an average of one to three strikes or "snaps," according to one study, to capture their prey. Some individuals prove much better shots than others.

If the basic pike strike falls into place early in life, so too does the northern's propensity for taking large prey, often noted in more colorful language when, for instance, a 5-pound northern grabs the legal walleye that is on your line and headed for your cooler. Pike measuring 19 to 20 millimeters have been observed catching and eating prey of 12 to 17 millimeters.

Pike have healthy appetites even at this stage of life. One study found that 3-inch pike ate at least one third of their body weight every day. Of course, a readily available food would replace an optimal food, the very definition of an opportunistic feeder. The study's pike fed on small items—plankton, for instance—during times of high light, the fry of other fish in the low light of dawn and dusk; they didn't eat after dark. This opportunistic pattern continues throughout their lives, as pike find bigger prey difficult to catch in bright light.

The best conditions for a healthy year-class of pike? Warm temperatures and high water, the combination of which has led to the recent explosion of pike numbers in reservoirs in Iowa, Colorado, and other western states. High water means that in-shore vegetation and setbacks enjoy enough depth to sustain the young-of-the-year pike; the warm temperatures mean plenty of food. One study found young-of-the-year pike numbers in these setbacks to be 3 times greater than the number of pike in emergent vegetation and 10 times the number of small pike in open bays. As it turns out, these little pike have every reason in the world to stay in those dense, shallow weeds.

## JUVENILE PIKE AND WEEDS

Young pike nearly always locate in or near some sort of concealment. The ability to remain unnoticed, first important when as larvae they hung vertically from weeds, continues as they grow. Emergent shoreline vegetation is vital to the survival of young pike, as shown by separate studies in New York's Oneida Lake, Lake Warniak in Poland, and Murphy Flowage in Wisconsin. In the Polish lake the introduction of phytophageous fish and carp led to a reduction of weeds, and pike numbers dropped. In Wisconsin the problem came in the form of a winter drawdown, which eliminated the aquatic vegetation. Little pike need these weeds as hideouts. Their chief concern? Bigger pike, which prefer foraging in deeper water and intermittent weeds.

*Big fish are cannibals* remains one of angling's enduring clichés. But cannibalism in northerns is no campfire fish story. In fact, as biologists are coming to realize, it is a central element in maintaining healthy pike populations. For whatever reason, pike anglers give cannibalism little serious play—it's sort of a family secret, even if the angling community has always unconsciously assumed cannibalism to be present. The Pikie Minnow, for instance, was the first "best plug" for pike, winning countless fishing contests during the 1930s, 1940s, and 1950s. The most popular color has always been the "pike color" that imitated vertical bars of a young northern. Its name, I suppose, suggests its intended mimicry. But aside from an oblique reference to a "pike color plug" in Ray Bergman's 1931 book, *Just Fishing,* I've never seen an explicit reference to the fact that it appears to imitate a young northern. In fact, early advertisements called the Pikie Minnow a killer plug for muskies and bass—as if *Pikie* were a name drawn from a hat.

This apparent paradox got me interested. Was this a case of anglers intuiting fish behavior ahead of field scientists? I researched the Pikie Minnow, even scouring the *Collector's Guide to Creek Chub Lures & Collectibles,* a book devoted to the history of the Creek Chub Bait Company, its lures, and the men and women who produced them. I learned the architecture of the Creek Chub factory, the sites of the annual company picnics, even the number of players on the Creek Chub Bait Company girls' basketball team of the 1930s. But I found no reference to the fact that the Creek Chub with natural pike colors worked (or was designed) because big pike like eating small pike. Now, the Creek Chub rose to fame in the late 1920s and early 1930s, between the early imitative ideas of Louis Rhead and the explosion of imitations for all species in the 1960s. After all, one of the most popular brook trout flies of the period was a Parmachene Belle, which was tied to look like the fin of a brook trout. Anglers may have simply assumed that cannibalism was so common that it didn't have to be noted. Maybe the whole matter is merely a case of my looking for explicit recognition of common knowledge. But check out the old decoys carved by pike spearers. You'll often as not see the form of small pike. I guess the point is not what inspired that design, what that representation meant then, but what it does now. I've got news for you: It's not like bigger pike are attracted to the wooden decoys because they're lonely and want to make friends.

*The veritcal lines of the Pikie Minnow match the markings of a juvenile pike.*

In any case, scientists today agree that pike begin eating one another at an early age, as early as one month. One observer of pike at the larval stage noted that feeding pike can catch and hold the smaller pike, thanks to their backward-curving teeth, but can do little more than kill them. (Pike are unable to ingest prey that constitute 70 percent or more of their body weight.) Still that didn't seem to deter them. Quite the opposite, in fact. At the beginning of the larval period only 3 percent of the pike in one study were cannibalistic; by the end of the larval period nearly 40 percent were. It may be that the vibrating tails of other pike elicit a feeding response. One researcher noticed that prior to feeding (in a tank), inch-long pike would line up and "make attacks on the vibrating tail of the other."

Pike in the 5- to 10-inch range try to forage where they are safe, but that isn't always possible. One bit of protection comes from the vertical bars that mark these smaller pike, which offer better protection in the inshore vegetation. The spots of adult pike offer better camouflage in the offshore weeds, where shafts of light lance through the leaves.

For years biologists believed that cannibalism occurred in the absence of other forage. Recent thinking suggests that on an individual level, cannibalism is less a last

*Pike eat each other whenever they can.*

resort and more a reflection of the pike's opportunistic nature. On a larger scale, cannibalism functions to keep the populations reasonably free of disease and the age structures in place. Other species of fish sustain populations with one trophic level eating fish of another level—cod, for instance. Certainly there are lakes in which pike survive (and do quite well) by eating themselves. In many pike waters the strength of one year-class of pike tends to be negatively related to the previous one, which in lay terms means that the big ones eat the small ones. Another scientific study review puts it thusly: "Even a very low cannibalism rate can cause significant mortality."

All of which underscores the significance of a diverse weed complex. Smaller pike require good hiding spots so they can wait for a meal to swim by. A substantial weeded area produces enough forage to allow that strategy to work. It has many "ambushing-hiding" spots so that smaller pike can use energy for attacking and catching prey, instead of saving their own skins. As one biologist concludes, "The poorer the vegetative habitat, the greater must be the spatial requirements of each individual."

Juvenile pike depend on the shoreline part of the weed complex because it provides a safe zone, as larger pike require cooler water. Again, a pattern is set early in a pike's life and continues into adult years: Hang out with other pike of the same size. To a pike, there's nothing better than, as Hannibal Lecter put it, having an old friend for dinner.

## ADULT PIKE AND WEEDS

Pike in tanks wait until the prey wanders within half a body length before striking. Pike in the wild likewise gain an advantage by attacking prey that's close to them, so they hang in or near some sort of weed growth. Pike will occasionally go on forays when prey species dwindle, but that strategy doesn't play to their strength as a predator.

Adult pike gravitate to areas where weed diversity is greatest. Such areas have baitfish, cooler temperatures, and more dissolved oxygen—creating, in essence, comfort and forage. In weedless waters pike use shoals and trees or boulders. One researcher found pike in the 16- to 24-inch range inhabiting this sort of cover near weedbeds, with bigger pike inhabiting the weeds themselves. Bigger fish get the better cover, not because they chase away the smaller pike, but in all likelihood because the smaller pike have the good instinct to keep out.

Weeds (and, in lieu of weeds, shoals, trees, and boulders) provide pike with shade, and beyond the comfort issue, the limited light makes attacking easier. It's like sitting in a darkened room: You can see out into a lighted room, but people in the lighted room can't see you. For a visual predator such as the northern, this advantage is important, particularly in warm water where repeated attacks without success deplete the fish's energy.

Best weeds? Adult pike do very well with pond-leaf or broad-leaf types. Pike hit on a line, so they need some space. Scattered or intermittent vertical stem cover lets them launch accurate attacks. They avoid the dense mats of vegetation like millfoil or coontail for this very reason. True, pike at times seem to hold tight to cover, usually during times of inactivity, but even then they nearly always attack toward deeper water.

## CURRENT MATTERS

For all the anthropomorphizing of pike as fierce and wild, they nearly always end up in slow current, preferring pools to riffles and runs. This selection represents more than simply avoiding current, which they could do by just staying in a slow section of the river. Rather, pike want to be in position to take advantage of the current's proximity, deriving oxygen from it, remaining in the breaks because adjacent flumes permit easy capture of disoriented baitfish. The base of a waterfall—which has deep water, oxygenation, and nearby current—is one of the best places to fish for big northerns.

A study of a Wisconsin river showed that smallmouths and northerns occupied the same segments of the stream, with northerns captured in areas where current velocity was low, aquatic vegetation present, and bank cover (fallen trees, stumps, beaver dams) available; smallmouths, on the other hand, were captured mostly in pools of moderate current with rubble and rock bottoms. In other words, bass and pike don't compete even though they share the same waters and even, to an extent, the same forage in terms of minnows and small panfish. Salmonids, smallmouth and largemouth bass, and walleyes—the other predator fish in cool-water regions—all use different habitats (or, in some cases, habitats differently), and most researchers find little evidence of competition for forage species.

Popular beliefs to the contrary, northerns seldom socialize with their *Esox* relatives. Muskies prefer current, and pike avoid it. Pickerel have a different range, and where they do overlap with pike, pickerel remain in shallow weeds year-round. Bigger waters like Lake of the Woods or Eagle Lake in Ontario or Leech Lake in Minnesota have sufficient habitat complexes to accommodate both pike and muskies, but most rivers or smaller lakes have one or the other *Esox* species.

The young-of-the-year *Esox* species do sometimes share habitat, and when that happens, northerns often come out on top. Pike spawn before muskellunge and produce greater numbers of young. The result? The young northerns feed on the smaller, younger muskies, although not by a selective design but simply because, like any smaller fish, the muskies become forage.

Meanwhile, the adult pike slowly recover from the stresses and strains of spawning as spring shatters winter's hold on the North Country. Water temperatures break into the 50s. Forage fish such as yellow perch, suckers, alewives, even small pike and exotic delicacies like stocked salmonids become available. Not that pike are fussy eaters. Stomachs rumble. Soup is on.

# PART II

## Spring, Late Spring, Early Summer

*This northern came from the inside lip of a bay, beneath some driftwood, a good spot for Canadian pike in the spring. Stan Warner.*

# 5

# Precious Metals

A month after the spawn, waters have warmed into the 50s and pike have recovered from their exertions and rediscovered their appetites. At no other time of the year do they feed so aggressively. The source of their foraging intensity is not, as we might have it, a case of hunger pangs after a sustained honeymoon, but rather a result of their invigorated metabolism and the availability of prey fish.

Pike hunt just outside marshy wetlands and tributaries, and in the adjacent shallow bays, flats, and shorelines that serve as transition zones between spawning areas and the main body of the lake, river, or reservoir. Yellow perch, suckers, alewives, chubs, shiners, and smelt mill around these areas recuperating from their own spawns. Northerns begin their banquet here in 3- to 10-foot flats, moving into transitional waters of 10 to 15 feet by June. Even in this spring season the bigger pike seem attracted to weedy shoals that rise from 10 or 20 feet to within several feet of the surface. From a northern's standpoint, such a place is as good as it gets: access to deep water, cool temperatures, a prime-time lair, and an all-you-can-eat buffet.

As spring progresses, pike show a general movement from shoreline trees and boulders and open bays to weed complexes. They make use of the cover as it becomes available, and a copse of weeds is always worth a cast or two—even in early May. If habitat is in short supply, the biggest pike will be there. After all, a few sprouts can offer camouflage and shade, crucial to effective predation.

## SPRING SPINNERS

Fishing had a seasonal flavor where I grew up in northern New York. Spring meant trout, except in the bays of Lake Ontario and the St. Lawrence River, where northerns ruled. And so that became pike fishing's time—the six weeks in May and early June after bullheading, but before the opening of bass season. Basically, when there was nothing else to catch or kill.

Most people who went pike fishing did so while they were doing something else—like putting in a dock or repairing the cottage. Take a break, make a couple of casts, see if the new dock will hold. Whoa, look at that, a pike!

My old friend Pete Bellinger and I used to fish these spring pike along the northern shore of Chaumont Bay, a broad, shallow tongue of eastern Lake Ontario. Back in the 1970s the lakeshore had very few year-round homes, and cottages were boarded shut until Memorial Day, at the earliest. No trout and salmon trollers back then, either. We'd wrestle the 15-foot aluminum boat down to the shore from the shed behind Pete's camp, clamp on an old 5-horse engine, hope it started, and, in a cloud of blue smoke, chug off into the emptiness of Chaumont Bay.

In retrospect this was a classic big-water spring pike spot: rock shores, sparse weed growth, 5- to 15-foot depths, clear water thanks to the shoreline lee. In all likelihood, the fishing was even better farther down in the bay, but we never trusted the clanky engine, and it was a long row back if it conked out. We'd let the wind push us halfway down the shore before starting back up, and we'd cast spinners like everyone else did for spring pike.

Back then, saying you had a selection of pike lures in your tackle box was like claiming you had a variety of dollar bills in your wallet. Spoons and spinners were the extent of the treasury, and in spring the Abu-Reflex was the coin of the *Esox* realm. The same company that manufactured the ubiquitous black Mitchell 300 spinning reels made the Reflex, and you always got a couple of free ones when you bought a reel.

I brought some suckers the first couple of times we went, but never got a hit on them. I tried Dardevles and Rapalas, too, but they caught only pre-spawn smallmouths. The pike wanted small spinners like ¼- to ⅛-ounce Panther Martins (silver blade, yellow body with red dots), Mepps (silver size 3 blade, squirrel tail), and Abu-Reflexs (silver blade, white body with black dots). Those were definitely our best lures.

We used trout gear, namely 5½-foot spinning rods with 6-pound-test line. We hooked some nice pike, too, fish that were a handful on light tackle. The boat would drift and rock in the waves, and the northerns would dive deep, twisting along the bottom. Boating them required a team effort, but we managed at least one or two in

*The in-line spinner is a top producer. This Lake Champlain northern took a white Roostertail on a blustery May morning. Matt Crawford.*

the 10- to 12-pound range on nearly every trip, and a couple of times we hooked pike even bigger than that.

The trick was to retrieve the spinner very slowly right along the drop-off, which fell from 8 to 12 feet and had a few scattered weedbeds. We hung up quite a bit on the rocky bottom, but if you worked your line from various angles, you could sometimes free the spinner. It was always a race between running out of line with the drift and getting the motor started. One time Pete got stuck on his first cast of the afternoon. It was windy, and we were drifting at a pretty good clip.

"You want to go get it?" I asked.

"Yeah, it's my only white Reflex," Pete said, loosening his buzzing drag. "Come on."

The outboard started on the second pull, and I turned the boat in the direction of Pete's line. But I didn't make much progress at first, and then it became clear why, as a spotted yellow-orange tail showed on the surface 30 yards off the bow. Pete looked at me, and we just started laughing.

Like most, this pike didn't run very far, and it wasn't long before we caught up to it. Pete worked the fish to the boat, almost within netting distance. The pike appeared at the surface in a swirl, and the dark green back of the great fish left me wishing for a bigger net. But the point became moot, as the pike dove beneath the boat and somehow pulled free.

I'd never seen a bigger pike, and I'd seen some pretty big ones. Pete reeled in his spinner and scrutinized it.

"Well, I caught part of him, anyway," he said. And I looked, and there on the barbs of one of the treble's hooks was the tiniest sliver of white flesh.

That was almost 25 years ago, and since then I've fished spring pike quite a bit. I still cast the Mepps size 3 blade when the fish are shallow and require slow presentations. Thomas Spinners, Canadian Spinners, Blue Foxes, and Roostertails make good choices, too. Keep them moving slow and steady along the bottom. Maybe it's analogous to spring training in baseball. Batters like their pitches grooved until they get their timing down—then they can handle curves, sliders, and knuckleballs. Perhaps spring pike want a nice easy pitch they can crush, too.

Northerns seem to prefer small lures during the first part of the spring. You'd think they'd want big imitations, given the adult status of the spring forage hanging around, but that just has not been my experience. Rather, I've come to rely on ⅛- to ½-ounce spinners early in the season. Later in spring when pike have begun to take up deeper positions, heavier spinners with quicker retrieves are in order. Roostertails in the ¾-ounce range hold their depth even at a good clip, making them ideal choices for the 10- to 15-foot-deep weedlines.

As for colors, silver blade/white body is a good clear-water combination, with silver blade/yellow or chartreuse body a second choice. I usually fish these spinners on 6-pound-test line and a light-action rod. You can cast them into the next zip code.

Drifting and casting is the best way to cover water. If the drift slides by too quickly, drag an anchor. Pike don't school, but they do concentrate in certain areas, and you don't want to blast through the best fishing. Pete and I favored one particular rocky point at the mouth of a cove, and we used to always anchor nearby. Even if we couldn't get a fish to hit, we could usually get one to follow. We'd drift off and return in an hour or so and sometimes get that pike to grab a spinner.

I was surprised how well spinners worked, to tell the truth. At the time I was a couple of years out of college, just starting to become interested in outdoor writing, and took the whole matter quite seriously. When I was fishing with Pete, I was "on assignment" for my $5-a-week column at the *Malone Evening Telegram* and considered it my journalistic duty to do some experimenting with different lures. But they didn't work. Even Dardevles.

This all became even more perplexing when I returned to Vermont, where I was living at the time, and started trying for spring pike on Lake Champlain. These pike wanted spinners, too. No spoons. Weird. At the time I was well into fishing tiny flies for rising trout, so I wasn't ready to confer the assignation of "selective" on pike, spots or not. Still.

## SPOONS

Some 15 years ago I found two guys who liked catching pike more than I did—Ray Coppinger and Stan Warner. One spring, the three of us went walleye fishing in the Bay of Quinte in southern Ontario. The first thing I noticed was that Ray and Stan both had spare rods rigged with wire leaders and spoons within their reach—as Ray explained, "in case a weedbed should slip up to the boat unannounced. The last thing you want to be doing is fumbling with your gear when you could be casting to a pike."

The walleyes proved difficult on the first morning, but Ray hooked and landed a nice northern by retrieving a spoon slowly and letting it drop. "It fluttered back past those weeds," he explained, releasing the pike, "and that's where the pike grabbed it." He dried his hands on his pants and let fly again.

Ray was using a blue and silver Cleo, so I clipped on a hammered-silver Cleo and started hooking pike, too. We did the best in one shallow, tributary delta—a great

*The Little Cleo is a terrific spoon. This pike took a stop-and-go flutter retrieve.*

spring spot, I realize now. A weedy shoal rose from 20 feet to within 4 feet of the surface. We'd approach this spot from deep water, knowing the pike would be hiding in the weeds.

My dad brought me up on trout-fishing etiquette—you never crowded, never cut in, never-ever cast to a fish that another angler was working. The proper thing to do was let the other person cast first while you complimented his form. Ray and Stan grew up with no such probations, and they'd be casting as soon as the shoal came in range. So much for politeness; I was letting fly with the best of them by the end of the trip. Often as not a pike would grab the first spoon that twinkled down through the depths. The challenge remained, however. You wanted to have the first spoon on the weed edge, but if you guessed wrong and cast too quickly, you covered nothing but open water, leaving the weed edge to your, uh, partners.

A bit of any angling is competitive, and if trout fishing manages to clothe it in a certain pastoral civility, pike fishing enjoys little in the way of such pretense. The competition is friendly, genuine, and celebrated, as in the smoky intensity of a barroom board game. Everyone cheers a good shot, for the joy of it. Mike Fink would have been one hell of a pike fisherman. I'm sure Ray and Stan would have welcomed him on their boat.

Since then I've come to use spoons in a number of spring (and summer) settings. They seem at their best along weed edges and defined weedbeds. The bigger the water, the better spoons work. On that trip with Ray and Stan the Bay of Quinte had a lot of alewives, and we were fishing in late May, just as the alewives were completing their spawning. Our pike probably mistook the silver Cleos for those alewives.

Spoons are the oldest of pike lures, evidence of bronze spoons dating to the 11th or 12th century in Europe. It's easy to see why they are so effective on pike. Whereas the spinner needs to be retrieved to work, the spoon never stops working—from the minute it hits the water and sinks and flutters to the time it comes wobbling to the boat. The *flip-flop-flip* of a spoon emits vibrations similar to those sent by a wounded minnow, so it appeals to pike not only on the visual level, but on a sonic as well. The tendency is to hurry the spoons along and cover the water, but a slow retrieve produces the best action. Try throwing the motor into neutral when trolling; or cast the spoon as far as you can and retrieve it in stops and starts, so that it darts past weedy hiding spots.

Trolling can be an excellent way to find spring pike, since the best locations in "early" bays are not always evident. If you can, navigate along a line of scattered weeds or depth change and keep your spoon in the 5- to 12-foot depths. You can catch pike trolling spinners, but add some swivels to reduce line twist. Spoons make better choices, especially if you work the rod as you troll.

My friends Mark Craig and Frank Flack troll for trout and walleyes along the same shores of Chaumont Bay that Pete and I used to drift years ago. They take some nice northerns in spring, but they're targeting lakers, so the water can't be that warm. One year they won a $1,000 prize in the spring fishing derby thanks to a 10-pound northern that hit a purple and white Evil Eye, which is a good name for a pike lure, I suppose, but is actually a lake trout spoon. As Mark recalled, "At first we were bummed because we'd thought we had a prizewinning brown on the line, but then Frank read the regs and we realized that the prize money for northerns was nothing to walk away from. We got to the weigh-in with the pike in good shape. Then, after he weighed the fish, the derby official grabbed the pike by the eye sockets and brought it back to us so we could release it."

Love those pike.

Which spoons are best? Fiords, Little Cleos, Blue Foxes, Dardevles, Red Eye Wigglers, Len Thompsons, Rapala weedless spoons, Johnson Silver Minnows, Thomas Buoyants, and Super Dupers—to name a few—all produce. The important part of your selection is to note the shape of the spoon: The wider it is, the greater the wobble and the heavier the sonic *thump.* Slender spoons produce a rocking motion. Most of my spoons are in the ¼- to ¾-ounce range, although I have some as large as 1 ounce, which I use in Canadian waters and in shallow, rough waters where the larger

*This angler works a spoon along a rocky shoreline, hoping to find a pike interested in feeding on some post-spawn baitfish.*

flash may be more visible, the heavier *thump* more noticeable. I have also used light trolling spoons to flutter retrieve in shallow water.

In general, choose silver and hammered silver in clear, open water; gold or brass in stained; and Fire Tiger in weeds. Chartreuse is a good general color. Red and white and Five of Diamonds (red on yellow) make attractive combinations, though they seem at their best in northern locations where pike see few lures. My friend Ray, who must have the world's biggest private collection of Cleo spoons, prefers a green or blue stripe over the silver. Whatever the choice, there's little cover in spring, so keep your tackle light—8- to 10-pound test is plenty. That way your lures will do their best dance.

## SPINNERBAITS

Some anglers begin the season casting spinnerbaits, but they always work better for me once the water temperature climbs into the high 50s and the weeds begin to grow.

My own rule of thumb is to start the day with an in-line spinner, at least during the spring and early fall. If weeds show at the top and/or the veggies seem to be sprouting randomly through an area, the spinnerbait is my choice out of the bullpen. And I have a quick hook. With its high-riding spinner and undulating skirt, the spinnerbait simply does a better shake and bake than the in-line spinner, which is less maneuverable and relies on a steady retrieve. You can pitch a spinnerbait into a hole in the weeds, then turn it down an alley and draw it back out to open water. And if a spinnerbait hits weeds, you can simply jerk it free. You can modify matters in midretrieve by letting the spinnerbait fall to a desired level and continuing your retrieve at a slow, steady pace. Or you can try a "go-and-stop" by retrieving the spinnerbait steadily at first, then slowing down as it passes a likely pike lair. If that doesn't work, accentuate the retrieve with some sharp twitches so that the skirt pulses through the water.

The spinnerbait loses something in open water. Some anglers think pike are more likely to chase a forage with a slim profile. Perhaps. And, perhaps that explains part of the appeal of the in-line spinner in scant cover, where it can be sighted for some distance. It may be a different matter in thick cover, where the blunt-shaped spinnerbait suddenly materializes in front of a hungry pike.

For spinnerbait color, make white your first choice in clear water and add a yellow or chartreuse trailer. If the water has a bit of stain to it, try yellow, chartreuse, or Fire Tiger. What about those realistic imprinted spinnerbaits? They work, too. But have I ever caught pike on them and not on white, yellow, or chartreuse? Nope.

*The spinnerbait earns its spots a bit later in the spring.*

Whereas in-line spinners and spoons can be effective even in the ⅛-ounce sizes, bigger is better with spinnerbaits. You want to push some water, send some vibes. More blades, bells, and whistles, too. I nearly always add a trailer, usually a plastic worm or twister, but sometimes a pork strip or the slender tails that Johnson markets to go with the Silver Minnow. A trailer slims down the overall profile of the lure, which may encourage more pike to go for it; the tail also adds a seductive wiggle and flutter, and gives the spinnerbait a chance to work more on its way down.

The spinnerbait may not be my first choice when the post-spawn fishing starts, but it is by the third week of fishing. My affection for it comes in part from how much fun it is to fish. Sometimes you'll feel several hits or bumps without hooking anything. Suddenly the vibration of the blade stops, the resistance on the rod wanes, and you feel an odd *click-click,* as if the spinnerbait is being pulled through the pike's mouth, which is just what's happening. If there's a trick to spinnerbaits, it is to set the hook as soon as you feel the *click*.

I am convinced that an attacking pike sometimes misses a bait on a sideways at-tack, which we feel as a bump. Then the pike reorients itself and overtakes the spin-

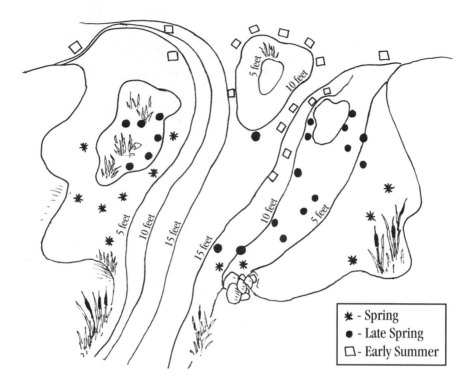

nerbait in a quartering rush, the preferred line of attack. The pike simply overswims it, which is why the initial sensation to the angler is one of nothingness and why the angler needs to reel and set the hook immediately.

## HARDWARE, THEN AND NOW

With all the modern emphasis on technology and the latest wonder lure, it's easy to overlook the pike-fishing insight of earlier generations. Even if most anglers fished pike rather casually, they still knew how. It's not like people woke up one day in 1995 and decided to start casting spoons and spinners for pike.

Like most anglers of his generation, my uncle Frank much preferred brook trout to northerns, but it was clear from his equipment and tackle box that he enjoyed all fishing. I'd pester him about which fish were his favorite, which lures worked best, and so forth. "Pike like red and white Dardevles," he told me. "Red Eye Wigglers are good, too, because they wobble like this in the water." He'd demonstrate with his hand. "Pike like things that shine, whirl, and snake along. You can't beat a spinner with a feathered tail, unless you add a pork rind or strip of perch belly. That will make it work even better."

He was in his 30s in the years after World War I, when the various approaches to pike fishing were beginning to congeal. His ideas reflected the thinking on pike in general, particularly with regard to the affinity pike had for spinners and spoons. A 1920 *National Sportsman* article by Dixie Carroll reveals the widespread use these artificials enjoyed. Carroll profiled 50 pike (between 12 and 29 pounds) caught between May and October in waters across the pike's range, from New York to Minnesota and from Indiana to Canada. At first glance the results appear so different as to seem quaint. Upon a closer investigation we see that the flash of silver (or nickel, as it was called) and copper (brass) was as important then as it is today.

Overall, 14 of the 50 pike were taken on plugs (anglers weren't necessarily fishing *for* pike when they caught one.) Twelve of the pike were caught on spoons (nickel outdid white and brass, 6 to 3 and 2, respectively), 10 on pork rind, 10 on minnows or chubs, 4 on frogs. Spinners aren't noted, in all likelihood because their use was so ubiquitous that the trailer was what distinguished the selections. Of the 10 successful minnows, 6 were rigged with spinners, while 9 of the 10 pork rinds were rigged with spinners.

In other words, 15 of the 20 minnow/pork rinds were rigged with spinners, which reflects one of the angling problems in fishing before spinning—keeping bait on the hook. But it also speaks to a productive presentation: erratic retrieves through shallow water and structure, alternately brisk and seductive, with a fluttering trailer. Much of what constitutes the spinnerbait's place in the modern pike angler's repertoire, in other words.

Today, of course, *a selection of pike lures* is no longer an oxymoron. Pike anglers can obsess about their choices like any other anglers and, as we will see in chapter 6, there are certain things to be imitated in pike fishing, though not always what lure manufacturers would have us think. For now we can say that pike fishermen have a wide range of artificials (and naturals), and over the course of a season each has its time to shine.

But spinners, spoons, and spinnerbaits remain the best lures you can snap onto your wire leader in the spring season, which pleases me to no end. I'd never use an old-time lure if a New Age artificial worked better. But I do love the old ones when they turn the trick.

They certainly do in May and early June. If you like fishing hardware, like the click of teeth on metal, this is your time. Nothing combs a bay like an in-line spinner, and nothing draws pike out of a growing weed bank or off a rocky point like a whirling blade or flopping slab of metal. The wink of silver seems to hold a special appeal for spring northerns. Perhaps pike are looking for the flash of schools of spawning baitfish. Perhaps pike lose their wariness over the winter.

Whatever the reasons, I find myself delighted by the northern's spring predilections. Just last May Stan Warner and I headed north for a day on Lake Champlain. Be-

*The shorelines of Great Lakes bays are terrific spring pike spots.*

fore we left, I phoned my friend Matt Crawford, editor of the *Burlington Free Press,* who planned to join us. "Fishing's been good," Matt said. "It's slime time. Looks like a front coming through, though." This made perfect sense, because Stan and I were going fishing, and that always produces a cold front.

We left Massachusetts at dinner, driving north through the verdant hills of southern Vermont. By the time we reached Burlington, the wind had shifted to the northwest. Hard. We could feel it buffet the van. At the motel we could see our breath, and we hurried inside to watch the Weather Channel: near-record cold, tomorrow—high 50 degrees, west winds 15 to 25 miles per hour, higher gusts. Terrific.

We met Matt the next morning at six and headed out. The wind pushed turbid water into the shores, and the weeds that had held pike for Matt three days before were clearly bereft of any gators now. We decided to nose our way around the point and work Goose and Gander Bays, which were protected from the wind. The way back was quite a ride, as we crawled up one wave and down another. I can still recall a wave breaking over the boat and Matt turning to me, with hair plastered like seaweed to his forehead, and allowing how "*that* was a 4-footer."

But in between we had some fishing to remember. Around midmorning the wind blew us offshore, and that's when we started to hit some good pike. Matt took a number of nice fish on white spinnerbaits, Stan took the biggest fish of the day—a 10-pounder—on a silver and white spoon, and I did respectably on white in-line spinners.

Somehow, that made me feel good. I mean, it just couldn't have happened to a nicer bunch of lures.

# 6

# Pike Foods, Pike Lures

The most consistent pike fishing of the season comes during the six to eight weeks following post-spawn recuperation. That is, late April, May, and June in the States and southern Canada, late May, June, and July as you work your way farther north. Northerns' daily food ration reaches a high point, as season-long studies find the lowest incidence of empty stomachs at this time of year. With water temperatures in the 50s and low 60s, pike can remain in fairly shallow water, where the hunting is good. And they certainly bring an enthusiasm to their work; their opportunism knows no bounds. When caught in Fyke (biological survey) nets, most gamefish regurgitate. Springtime pike often as not use the opportunity to tank up on available prey.

## A LEAN, MEAN EATING MACHINE

Predation starts with exceptional vision. In the words of one researcher, "The composition and structure of the retinal photoreceptors of northern pike is typical for a fish with good vision in clear light." Pike have considerable eyeball mobility, permitting them to see in any direction and track fast-swimming baitfish. They can judge distance and depth thanks to the "veritable sighting groves on their snouts in front of their eyes."

Although vision remains the prime tool of feeding, it is not by sight alone that they live. In one experiment, blinded pike were able to catch living prey in tanks by reacting strongly to "mechanical stimuli" (vibrations) as long as they were within 2 to 5 inches of the prey. Interestingly, "In comparison to pike with normal vision, blinded pike seemed to capture prey fish faster." The significance of lateral line was underscored by samplings in the Dutch Kleine Wielen that turned up the same blind pike for three successive years. As one report concludes:

> The sense organs are more developed on the head of the pike than on the rest of the body. This indicates that the lateral sense organ is of primary importance in prey capture behavior of the pike. Olfactory organs, so important during mating, are virtually unimportant during feeding. Water flows through the folds only when the fish is moving, which may explain why fish in the spring, which are moving, do seem to respond to dead baits which have been in the same area for awhile and thus give off considerable odour.

The actual mechanics of the strike remain unchanged from the first year of life. Pike seem most successful when striking from the rear and side, in a sort of quartering angle. A 90-degree angle gives the prey a better chance at avoiding the strike, as it requires the most precise lead. Pike strike at the center of the prey's mass and do so with maximum acceleration. Both their mucus and their cylindrical shapes minimize friction and enhance speed during the attack—another key ingredient in their feeding strategy.

After singling out the target, pursuing it, and propelling itself with a snap from the S-position, the pike keeps its mouth closed until the final moments, thus building up pressure that creates a vacuum and sucks in the prey. Adult pike can attack from a distance of 30 feet, but closer strikes generate quicker acceleration, more vacuum-building pressure, and a greater likelihood of success.

A northern's quick acceleration means that it can miss or overshoot its target, in part because the positioning of its fins at the rear prevents effective braking. Thus the pike's feeding dilemma: The stalk, pursuit, and accelerating S-strike add up to a terrific technique when the pike hits the mark, but end up a liability if the initial lunge misses. On the other hand, the pike's swirl and resulting turbulence can disorient a baitfish, thus creating the opportunity for a second strike if the first is missed.

Whereas some fish school in order to flush prey to one another, pike feed on their own—their morphology is cylindrical, in contrast to the compact body shape of bass. The latter can twist and turn quickly and intercept prey flushed in the right direction. Pike appear distracted—perhaps overexcited—by such peripheral activity. They're riflemen, not scattergunners. They must zero in on a particular target.

## PREY AVOIDANCE

It's not like small fish swim around trying to get eaten. Bluegills, for example, rely upon a dart-freeze maneuver. Other species hide in the weeds or dive to the bottom. Open-water baitfish swim in schools, which often elicits false starts from pike, a sort of flock-shooting syndrome. Studies show that a pike's predation success decreases as prey density increases. The school unifies in the presence of a northern, scatters as the pike attacks, then reunifies in the aftermath. Interestingly, these mirror-sided, open-water baitfish depend on sunlight for camouflage; without the light, their "mirrors" don't reflect background but instead reveal their outlines, which is why you'll see panfish and gamefish in shade—beneath a dock, say—but shiners milling in the sun. Without sun, their defense changes. Research on spottail shiners, a common open-water prey, shows schools dispersing in low light. As a result, late afternoon becomes a time of increasing vulnerability, particularly for those shiners on the outlying edges of the school, which the study found are most vulnerable to pike attacks.

Schooling is only one defense. In a fascinating 1969 study, researchers observed an alarm reaction in blinded minnows after contact with water in which a pike had

*The mirror sides of this baitfish permit it to use a bright daylight and schooling behavior to avoid predation. Or try anyway.*

captured and eaten a small minnow. However, these same minnows exhibited no such alarm reaction to water in which a large minnow had swallowed a small roach. The conclusion? The sharp teeth of the northern punctured the skin of the minnow, causing an alarm enzyme to disperse in the water. In another study, Atlantic salmon smolts reacted instinctively with prey avoidance behavior upon the very presence of a pike in the tank. Interestingly, these smolts were, in the words of a researcher, "predator in-experienced" and exhibited no such prey avoidance behavior upon seeing burbot.

## FAVORITE FOODS

Pike feed opportunistically. In essence, a predator with a waiting, ambushing hunting strategy has no other choice. The relative abundance and seasonal availability determine the prey species. In a study conducted on Heming Lake in Canada, trout-perch represented the most important forage during May and June; spottail shiners during July; yellow perch during August; sticklebacks during September and October. Northerns foraged infrequently on ciscoes, except during cold-water months. Again, the key variable appears to be the extent to which various prey species were available—and vulnerable—to northerns.

In recent years much has been made of northerns' purported interest in soft-finned, high-protein forage. True or false? Good question. A 1978 study conducted on eastern Lake Ontario found that pike favored alewives over white and yellow perch, in spite of the fact that the latter were more abundant. Another study found pike rejecting and avoiding sticklebacks more than other minnows due to "a non-conditional response to the strong mechanical stimuli caused by the spines" and a learned response to visual stimuli that "cause the pike to avoid sticklebacks before they have even touched them."

Laboratory experiments reached similar conclusions. Gizzard shad, carp, big-mouth buffaloes, fathead minnows, and smallmouth bass were considered highly vulnerable to pike predation. In contrast, green sunfish, pumpkinseeds, largemouth bass, and yellow perch were considered to be of intermediate vulnerability, and channel catfish, northern pike, bluegills, and black bullheads were considered of low vulnerability. Yes, laboratory conditions, but the general trend of "armament discouraging predation" seems to hold.

Over the years research as well as fishing wisdom have therefore concluded that northerns prefer cylindrical, soft-finned baitfish to spiny centrarchids, ostensibly because the ciscoes, alewives, shiners, and suckers offer high protein and tender victuals. One study found that pike took white suckers and gizzard shad and other

*A good population of shiners permit pike to grow large.*

soft-finned fish in preference to yellow perch. Along the same lines, a 1971 study found that two-year-old pike continued to feed on tadpoles, crayfish, and larvae even though the pond had an abundance of bluegills. Subsequent studies of tiger muskies and bluegills drew similar conclusions. Finally, a 1967 research project carried out by the Indiana Department of Natural Resources compared northern pike, chain pickerel, grass pickerel, walleyes, and channel catfish as predators of bluegills. Northerns were considered the least effective. These findings, in short, all support the spines-put-off-pike theory.

An impressive 1988 study conducted at Ohio State University concluded as much: "Esocids [northern pike] grew more slowly when centrarchids [bluegills] were the only prey than they did when gizzard shad were available." When both were available, "Esocids strongly preferred gizzard shad over bluegills. To maximize growth and survival, esocids should be stocked in systems with soft-rayed or fusiform prey, such as cyprinids [minnows] or shad, rather than centrarchid-dominated systems." That sounds pretty conclusive, but as the old saying goes, the devil is in the details, and in particular the details regarding the reason why.

The Ohio State study compared how pike preyed on bluegills, fathead minnows, and gizzard shad. As predicted, pike had the most success catching and eating fathead minnows and gizzard shad. But it isn't as if the pike didn't *want* to catch the bluegills; rather, they couldn't. Per experiment, they actually attacked more bluegills than they did the other two forage species, but caught fewer of them. Pike spent much more time following and pursuing the bluegills—"energetically costly behaviors," in the words of the researchers. A bluegill capture required five times as many strikes as did a fathead minnow or gizzard shad capture. Not only did pike catch fewer bluegills, but they lost more of the ones they managed to snatch because they grabbed them by the head or the tail rather than in the midbody region, which would permit a secure hold. The researchers believe the aiming adjustment was due to the spines.

Bluegills have successful strategies for avoiding pike predation, in other words. Researchers emphasize their dart-and-freeze escape pattern, their quick acceleration, their smaller turning radius. As the study reports: "In contrast to these anti-predator behaviors, fathead minnows and gizzard shad relied exclusively on schooling to avoid predation."

As a result, pike preferred fathead minnows and gizzard shad, but actually spent more time trying to eat bluegills—which sounds like a paradox until you consider that *anglers* use the term *preference* to indicate desire or want, while *biologists* use it in reference to the actual amount of forage consumed. It is clear in this study that pike "preferred" fathead minnows and gizzard shad in a biologist's lexicon, but not in an angler's. The point? Pike populations do better with a forage base of cylindrical, soft-finned prey. Pike expend less energy chasing them and can catch bigger specimens, so they grow faster. In human terms, these prey are better for them. But as with humans, this doesn't mean that pike necessarily *want* to eat them, given a choice. In short, bluegills may make a poor forage base for a lake and offer a reasonable—one could even argue, superior—basis for imitation in an artificial lure.

Is there ever a time when a pike would try for one prey species and not the other? I think so. A predator can't risk missing a lot of first strikes, because it will end up losing energy instead of gaining it. So pike do have to "decide" if they can capture prey with one shot, particularly during warm-water months, when energy levels are low. What if suckers have not only soft fins but also less effective avoidance tactics—such as sinking to the bottom and remaining motionless? For a predator like a pike, which relies on its vision, that sucker is simply dinner waiting to happen. In other words, there may well be times when pike target open-water baitfish such as smelt, alewives, whitefish, and ciscoes not because they taste better, but because they have less effective escape strategies.

As an angler, it's difficult to let go of the idea that pike go after chubby, soft-finned suckers because they find them yummier than spiny, heavily scaled bluegills.

*Pike "prefer" soft-rayed baitfish not because they taste better but probably because they are easier to catch.*

I've always thought that way, to tell the truth. Part of me, I suppose, still does. But a predator like a pike lives on the edge of an energy equation that shifts with its growth, available forage, and water temperature. Living for a delicious meal rather than an easy one constitutes a luxury an adult pike just can't afford.

These factors probably explain the pike's appetite for more exotic foods. We judge "exotic" by species, whereas pike do so by behavior and availability. From a pike's standpoint, frogs represent an exotic food. How often do you see one swimming over a 10-foot drop-off? We see them all the time in the shallow weeds as we're launching the boat, so it's easy to think of them as common pike forage, particularly with their reputation as an excellent bait. In fact, European writers often note (historically and presently) the antipathy between the species. But frogs seldom show up in a pike's diet, except occasionally during the post-spawn when pike are in shallow water, and during early fall when the frogs migrate from the shallows to mud bottoms. The reason, I'm sure, has to do with the availability of the frogs to the pike.

Many anglers consider ducklings to be a favorite menu item of pike (a popular image, thanks to magazine photos and covers as well as declining midcentury waterfowl populations). A fascinating 1945 study on the Saskatchewan River delta found that approximately 1 percent of the pike examined contained young waterfowl in their stomachs. Predation on waterfowl was found in about half the areas in the Canadian provinces, though again this would probably not be the case in the southern part of the pike's range, where other foods are more available and pike are likely to be in deeper water during summer "hatches." In the southern part of the range, in other words, ducklings would be an exotic forage. At certain times in the northern part of their range, ducklings would be anything but.

Do pike select certain sizes of forage fish? Probably not. A 1960 research project conducted on Rybinsk Reservoir in the former Soviet Union found pike prey to range from 1¼ to 6 inches. Certain size ratios (between prey and pike) do make for the most efficient foraging. More recent data suggest that prey one quarter the size of the predator is optimal. However, as pike get bigger, they show a relative decrease in the size of prey consumed—which makes sense, as even 20-pound pike don't go looking for schools of 5-pound smallmouths, but may well keep an eye out for a single walleye in the 2-pound class. Also, the poorer the prey avoidance behaviors, the larger the size of prey that pike can go for—which is why they eat bigger shad than bluegills, for instance.

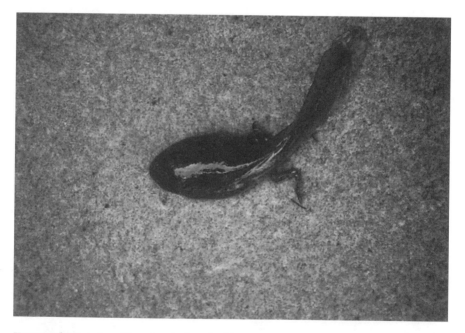

*Young pike occasionally eat tadpoles, ducklings, crayfish, muskrats and other foods they encounter, but most of their diet involves whatever fish they can catch.*

As pike grow, they simply can't risk the energy loss that comes from launching unsuccessful attacks. So their foraging becomes more conservative, in a sense. Larger pike spend most of their lives with empty stomachs. In one study, no pike in the oldest age group contained more than two prey fish. A 1984 study suggested pike growth was greater when pike spent more time digesting, less time chasing, which fits with the commonly held belief that big pike eat big prey. To which I would add, "When they can." More likely, they eat the prey they know they can catch—not so dramatic, I know, but closer to reality.

## ELEMENTS OF SUCCESSFUL LURES

All of which seems strangely congruent with the myths humans have constructed about pike as indiscriminate eating machines. Nothing is safe—from ducklings to mule's lips to the trailing fingers of canoe campers. It's true. Pike feed on what is abundant and available. In short, whatever crosses their path.

And the prey doesn't even have to wiggle or look like it's alive. Scavenging for a meal is fine by big pike. We value great northerns for their dramatic, crashing strikes. But they'd just as soon kick over a few garbage cans. In separate experiments conducted in Heming Lake, Minnesota, Loch Choin, Scotland, and elsewhere, researchers made an initial application of rotenone to ponds, which weakened the small pike but not the larger ones. As a result, the small pike were prostrate on the surface, dying if not dead. In every case, the big pike moved right in to snap them up.

While Rome burned! These, the vicious, fearless predators of myth and legend.

Herein lies the pike's vulnerability, so to speak. They're suckers for an easy meal, a handout. One study found inefficient prey avoidance behavior very important in eliciting pike attacks, more important than the color, brightness, size, or shape of the prey. In that respect, we can say that pike do select, albeit for vulnerability. Is there such a thing as a "pike action" that suggests prey vulnerability? Absolutely.

## ACTION

The flashy wobble of a spoon no doubt suggests a fish having trouble swimming on line, just as the spin of a blade on a stem or swivel suggests a slowly swimming baitfish or perhaps, with the accompanying flash and turbulence, a baitfish joining others in an attempt to avoid predation by schooling.

The side-to-side shimmy of a plug resembles the swimming motion of an injured baitfish or minnow, too. A deeply hooked perch swims off with an exaggerated motion in which its entire body gyrates. No doubt plugs and, as discussed in chapter 5, spinners and spoons send out vibrations similar to this perch.

In visual terms, nothing reproduces the struggle of a wounded baitfish like the wriggle of a twister tail, plastic worm, or rubber minnow, or the flutter of a pork rind strip, a strip bait, or even a free-sinking spoon. A plummeting jig may well trigger a strike in a different way, as pike prey often attempt to avoid capture by diving into the rocks or grass.

The pulse, an action which comes from the skirt of a spinnerbait or from the breathing motion of a marabou streamer or feathers on a jig, has a real appeal. This action suggests life within a form or, in terms of predator avoidance, the freezing strategy. If the pulse is motion within the form of a stationary lure, the glide or dart is the overall movement bereft of motion within its form. This action seems a deadly imitation of a minnow or baitfish unaware of its impending demise. Soft jerkbaits such as Slug-Gos and jerkworms, hardbodies such as Rattlin' Rogues and Zara Spooks—in effect a floating jerkbait—all provide this action, which is in fact the arresting absence of movement.

Some final thoughts on this matter of action. Anglers often encounter pike as they rush for a lure, which is why pike have the reputation of preferring (in an angling sense!) speedy lures. True, you can sometimes get a following pike to take by hurrying your lure, but you can just as often get the fish to take by changing the lure's direction, slowing down, stopping, or stopping and restarting your retrieve.

In general, pike size up prey and go for the ones they have the best shot at catching with one pass. If you miss a pike, slow your retrieve slightly and be ready for a return strike. Pike are used to wounding quarry then finishing it off with a second or third try, as was evident in the Ohio State study. If there's no follow-up strike, try casting to the same spot with a lure that permits an even slower presentation. For example, if a pike makes a pass at a buzzbait and misses, put a Zara Spook back in the same spot; if a pike misses a spinnerbait, try a plastic worm or jerkbait. Largemouth bass anglers popularized this trick, but it works for pike, too.

At times pike do like a little speed, usually on the surface. Skittering is a good example. Buzzbaits catch pike, too, but they seem at their best when worked a little slower than you might for largemouths. In fact, pro bass fishers often speed up their lures to keep them away from the pike. At times pike do want a steady speed at the 10-foot depth, which can be accomplished with either a deep-running plug or a heavy in-line spinner.

The best lures combine several actions. Most spoons, for instance, really wobble and glide. A Johnson Silver Minnow with a pork rind offers a wobble or rocking motion and a flutter. A marabou streamer with saddle hackle tails has both a breathing action and a fluttering action, and if retrieved in strips, it will dart and glide as well. A spinnerbait has the pulsing of the skirt and the spinning of the blade, and most anglers add a fluttering trailer to dress it off. Like other lures, a spinnerbait also brings to the table an appeal to the pike's lateral line, so it works on multiple levels.

These "revelations" may well seem a little underwhelming to experienced pike anglers. In fact, the art of pike fishing involves how to match these actions with pike mood and location, both of which change with conditions and the seasons. For now it is enough to note that pike imitations really do imitate, even if it is a particular behavior rather than species of forage that remains the point of the ruse.

## COLOR

Clear water usually calls for the following color choices (in *descending* order): white, silver, gray, pale olive, fluorescent yellow, chartreuse, blue, red. The choice for flash in clear water starts with silver/chrome and then turns to copper. Dark or turbid water calls for color choices as follows: fluorescent yellow, chartreuse, fluorescent orange, red and white. For flash, copper, gold, silver, in that order.

Most lures come in some sort of combination of colors. Often as not I start with white or yellow, silver flash, and a splash of orange and red. White has been my most effective pike color over the years, with the exception of top-water lures, which seem to do better in greens, olives, and oranges. In clear waters I lean toward more natural combinations (Creek Chub's pike color, Rapala Minnow, blue on silver), and if the water has a bit of a stain, I would probably start with Fire Tiger (chartreuse/fluorescent yellow/fluorescent orange). In shallow, thick cover I've begun working Fire Tiger into the rotation pretty quickly, regardless of water clarity. Finally, I believe in color contrasts. Many of the best pike lures have strong separations—black and silver, black and gold, red and white, Five of Diamonds (red on yellow), and so forth.

The above represent tendencies, and in fact the whys of color choice remain rather mysterious. After all, pike have no species preferences when it comes to forage, but the fact remains that a white spinnerbait is probably the top all-around pike lure in the waters I fish. White, bright, and flashy, it exemplifies the common thinking that pike chase what is most visible, though to be honest the "simpleton fish—bright trinket" theory has always seemed a bit too easy. It's not like pike have much trouble seeing suckers, and they're about as drab as can be. I think there's something more to it. I think color must relate to prey behavior, given how much it matters.

Several years ago I got into an over-the-counter discussion with Martha's Vineyard striper wizard Cooper Gilkes III, who explained why white flies work for stripers: "Imagine a big old striper laying down there in the surf. Well, he looks up and there's an easy white belly flopping around."

"So the striper knows it can catch the bait," I said, an eager if not particularly gifted student.

"I'd say that's a fair statement, Captain." And it occurred to me maybe that's what goes on with pike and white—that white is the color of vulnerability.

In other words, when a pike sees a dark color, it registers a prey fish swimming upright. But when it sees a light color with corresponding flash, a pike registers a prey fish on its side and in trouble. This would certainly explain why pike prefer light colors (white, yellow, chartreuse, orange) to the olives, purples, and blacks: The former are the colors of prey stomachs. This theory would also explain why dark colors work well on top-water lures in that the dark back suggests a prey fish on its side, as it would be flopping on the surface. Finally, this idea perhaps explains the effectiveness of the contrasting light and dark colors that mark some of the most famous pike lures of all time: The flipflopping of light and dark could well mimic a fish attempting to right itself as it swims out of danger.

## SHAPE

If vulnerability can be implied through action and color, it can be further evoked through lure shape. The research concludes that prey shape doesn't matter, but I'd just as soon go with a shape that pike know they are likely to catch. And that means thin, fusiform, or soft-finned forage such as smelt, shiners, ciscoes, chubs, suckers, and, yes, little pike and trout. At a distance a slim profile might just look like food more than some other object. Most pike lures, be they spoon, spinner, plug, or plastic, present such a profile. As research indicates, pike in and around weedbeds may be more inclined to try to catch blunt-shaped bluegills, which could account for the success of spinnerbaits as you get thicker into weeds. I often try to extend the rounded shape of the spinnerbait by adding a trailer. Of course, there are any number of slender lures—stickbaits, for example—that work just fine in weedy areas. In any case, the point may be that shape matters more in open water. And if we want to edge out farther on this speculative branch, we might wonder whether a thin shape be-

*Stan Warner's foam solution to the pike angler who can't make up his mind and who wants his lures handy but out of the way of flopping pike.*

comes most important on surface lures because of the strong silhouette that emerges when a lure is viewed against the sky.

## NOISE

Pike have a lateral line sensitivity, as shown by the study that looked at effective predation of the blinded pike. Whether the source is the thump of a spoon, hum of a spinner, or steady whisper of a plug, vibrations matter because they suggest a struggling prey. Some anglers believe that rattles attract pike. Others think they scare them. I'm not so sure about all lures, but I do think that noise can be important in surface lures. Perhaps noise above the water suggests feet or fins slapping on the surface, again emitting the vibrations of vulnerability. The same bag-of-bolts noise below the surface may suggest less vulnerability than artificiality.

## SIZE

I usually start with bass-sized lures except in wilderness fishing situations, which call for a bigger size. When trolling, I'll also up the size a notch. At times, particularly in weedy areas with rough water, I have seen a big spoon outfish a small one, possibly because the flash was more visible. When the sun is high and the water clear, dropping down a size or two doesn't hurt, either. Research suggests that pike of all age-classes tend to decrease the size of their prey as light intensifies. Pike that don't have the energy to catch bigger baits will often look to fill up on smaller ones, which are slower to escape.

## TEXTURE

A vulnerable-appearing texture never achieves the importance it does with artificials designed for walleyes, smallmouths, and largemouths. That said, soft jerkbaits occasionally do work when nothing else will, especially on the heels of a cold front. Part of their success no doubt depends on the fact that they fish well when worked very slowly near cover.

## SCENT

As research shows, pike don't rely on smell much at all—certainly not the way catfish or largemouth bass do. Smell might matter in the pre-spawn and immediate post-spawn, when pike feed on about-to-decompose winterkills, and when dead bait on the bottom works. Pike need to move in order to smell, which only strengthens the case for dead baits on migrating spring pike.

## THE MODERN PIKE TACKLE BOX

If the issue with northerns is being able to imitate a range of prey behaviors rather than prey types, which lures and tackle make the most sense?

After all, with the growing awareness of pike-fishing methods, there are now many more pike lures than ever before. And being fully aware that I'm probably better off giving my boss unsolicited marriage advice than I am telling fishermen what lures they need, here is my list of essentials:

- **Spoons**—Silver; silver and blue; copper or gold; red and yellow; chartreuse. Try to get some different shapes (wide to narrow), and weights from ¼ to 1 ounce.

- **Weedless spoons**—Fire Tiger (Johnson or Rapala).

- **In-line spinners**—Silver blade and white body; silver blade and yellow body; silver blade and chartreuse body; silver blade and red body. Dressing should be squirrel tail, bucktail, or hackle the color of the body or darker (such as black dressing, red body). Sizes from ⅛ to 1 ounce, including at least one or two muskie models.

- **Spinnerbaits**—Silver blade and white body; silver blade and yellow body; silver blade and chartreuse body; gold blade and yellow body; gold blade and chartreuse body; Fire Tiger blade and body; gold blade and orange and brown body.

- **Surface lures**—Jitterbug or Crazy Crawler; Pop-R or Chug Bug; Smithwick's Devil's Horse or Dying Flutter; Sputterbuzz, Zara Spook; buzzbait. Natural colors such as gray, silver, gold, brown, yellow, and stripes are all top producers. At times fish may want more vibrant combos such as Fire Tiger.

- **Plugs (shallow)**—Rapala, Mann's Minus One, Pikie Minnow, Big-O, or Fat Rap. For colors, see Surface Lures.

- **Plugs (medium deep)**—Shad Rap or C.C. Rattlin' Shad; Wally Diver; Bomber; Mann's Stretch (20 or 25). For colors, see Surface Lures.

- **Jigs**—Lead heads from ¼ to 1 ounce, dressed with marabou and bucktail in white, yellow, and chartreuse.

- **Plastic worms (8 inch)**—Fluorescent yellow, black, red, and violet with firetail.

- **Twister tails**—White, chartreuse, fluorescent orange.

- **Jerkbaits (hard)**—C.C. Rattlin' Rogue; Rapala Husky Jerk. For colors, see Surface Lures.

- **Jerkbaits (soft)**—Silver sparkle and flesh, gold sparkle and flesh, sparkle and chartreuse.

- **Flies**—Dumbbell or stick-on eyes; marabou hackle (wound) with mixed yellow and white saddle hackle tail; Dahlberg Diver tie with same marabou and saddle hackle tail; Berryman and Reynolds Bunny Fly.
- **Pork strip**—White.
- **Hooks**—1/0 weedless.

## TACKLE AND GEAR

Pike fishing requires certain bits of gear, most of which center upon handling pike. You need a good-sized net or fish cradle to assist with landing bigger fish. You definitely need a pair of needle-nose pliers for extracting hooks. A pair of jaw spreaders can give you the necessary operating space.

Like any normal angler, I don't have anywhere near the number of rods I need. Mine range from a light-action spinning rod with 6-pound test that is also suitable for smallmouths to a heavy baitcaster with 20-pound test that doubles as a backup winch for my truck.

My light-action outfit sees most of its use with spoons and jigs offshore in deep water where there is little danger of losing a fish in brush or weeds. I can point to no evidence that pike are in any way "leader" shy, but the lighter line does give a more natural flutter to a dropping lure and lets crankbaits run deeper.

I have two in-between outfits, one a medium spin outfit spooled with 8- to 12-pound test, the other a light baitcaster with 10-pound test. These rigs meet most pike-fishing situations. They handle plastics and other light lures as well as spinnerbaits, plugs, and spoons, and they absorb the thrashing of bigger northerns, too. I also like to have on board a medium baitcaster with 14- or 17-pound test and a medium-heavy baitcaster with 20-pound test for throwing big-time plugs, spoons, and spinnerbaits, particularly when working thick cover.

I'd actually rather fight pike on heavier tackle, because they respond so violently to the pressure. It is fashionable to say that the 3- or 4-pounders are great fun on light tackle—and they are in open water. In weedy water the light tackle becomes a pain, because the pike wrap around weeds and you usually have to paddle over and dig them out. The whole scene ends up being no fight at all until you get the pike in the boat, which is not where I like to battle fish. The fight of a 4-pound fish in weedy water is enhanced by a stubby baitcasting rig that takes it to them.

Pike fight in lunges and bursts, which is one of the reasons they twist the leader and break tackle. They elude predators like you and me in much the way they attack

*Needle nosed pliers are an essential part of the pike angler's gear.*

prey—in short, ferocious fits. They neither dog like a walleye nor thump like a bass. While some of their leaps are absolutely spectacular, they tend to thrash more than spring. They virtually never run much line.

Occasionally, I get the sense that larger pike may not even realize the danger of being hooked. That changes when they see Mr. Boat Net and everything goes directly to hell. This is how rods get broken. Stout tackle lets you pressure the fish from the start. The pike will respond earlier and thus be less energized at boatside. If the pike decides on a late-round rally, the heavy tackle affords some latitude.

Big pike will roll on lines and bite them off, but I usually avoid the heavy, longer leaders and stick with a 6-inch wire leader and 20-pound test, unless I'm fishing sur-

*A medium-light baitcaster is a terrific outfit for many pike situations.*

face plugs or flies or casting over bass (in which case I use lighter shock leaders; see chapters 8 and 9). I do buy a lot of wire leaders, however, as they become twisted after hauling in a few fish. Terminal tackle choices depend upon the size of the pike you are likely to catch and how you are fishing for them. You often hear how pike "smash tackle," but much of this is angling hyperbole that comes from bringing in a green fish too quickly. Sure, they will destroy a spinnerbait, but some of my best pike plugs are 10 years old. I once caught 12 pike on the same soft jerkbait. Terminal tackle, in short, mostly matters in the wilderness, where pike are bigger and more abundant, and where you can't just run out and buy another chartreuse spinnerbait.

The above ideas on pike imitations and tackle certainly didn't start with me, but rather have emerged over time, particularly in the last 20 years. Through the early and mid–20th century writers such as Ray Bergman, A. J. McClane, and others began to outline pike tactics. Kit Bergh's 1975 book *Northern Pike Fishing* remains a landmark today. I'm not sure how many copies it sold, but his thinking about pike was way ahead of its time. The *In-Fisherman* group published one book (*Northern Pike Secrets*) that offered an intriguing look at the seasonal nature of pike and how to catch them. Dick Sternberg's 1992 book *Northern Pike and Muskies* remains a beautifully illustrated, clearly written outline of *Esox* tactics.

*In-Fisherman* magazine consistently publishes first-rate how-to articles on virtually every aspect of northern pike fishing, blending a scientific understanding of pike with field-tested methods. Good articles also appear in regional magazines. Rod Teehan has written some very good pieces in the New England edition of *The Fisherman,* for instance. In 1996, a Michigan angler named Joe Bednar formed Pikemasters, a group devoted to pike conservation and recreation. Its newsletter offers the latest on pike methods, with certifiable pike crazies revealing secret strategies—for example, how to mute the rattles on that favorite plug that swims great but makes too much noise. Have you ever wondered why someone didn't combine a spoon and a spinnerbait? Well, they did, and you can buy one from an advertisement in this newsletter.

The point is that North American pike fishing does not enjoy a venerable literary tradition, certainly nothing like European pike fishing or American fly fishing. But it has begun to develop a body of literature that explores pike behavior, outlines effective fishing strategies, and cultivates an appreciation of pike as gamefish. That treatment has a way to go, certainly, but it's also been a long time coming. We need to recognize steps when we take them.

# *Pike Lures and Flies*

1. Crazy Crawler 2. Dying Flutter 3. Rapala 4. Baby Pike 5. Bass 'n' Shad 6. Mann's Stretch

1. Dardevle  2. Rooster Tail  3. Spin 'n' Spoon  4. Red Eye Wiggler  5. Mepps Musky Killer  6. Little Cleo

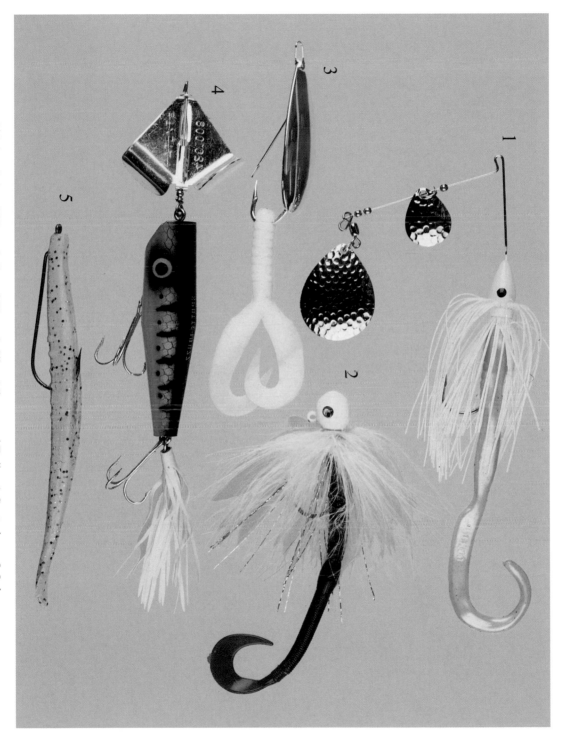

1. Spinnerbait and Worm  2. Jig and Worm  3. Silver Minnow and Trailer  4. Sputterbuzz  5. Jerkworm

1. Marabou Pike Streamer  2. Sparkle Grub  3. Jig and Worm  4. Marabou Matuka  5. Dahlberg Diver  6. Little Pike
Note: When fished, the Sparkle Grub and the Jig and Worm ride hook up.

# 7

# All the Right Moves

In a pike's world, late spring–early summer represents a time of plenty. Energy for hunting, with 60-degree temperatures in the shallows. Cover for hiding, with weedbeds and weedlines forming. And forage for dining pleasure, with baitfish and panfish spawning and recuperating along the shorelines

You won't find 20-pounders in 2 feet of water as you might have a month ago, but you should find plenty of adult pike patrolling the growing weeds in 5 to 15 feet of water. Smaller fish up to 5 or 6 pounds continue to hold in shallows, might do so right through midsummer in fact, depending on the forage. Bigger pike will almost always set up operations along the deepest available weeds, however, from now through September.

The fishing changes, too. Plugs and other full-bodied minnow imitations become increasingly productive through this period. Many anglers do just fine fishing nothing more than spinners and spoons, and if I absolutely had to catch a pike, I'd be sure I had a white spinnerbait with a yellow and orange trailer in my tackle box when I left the dock, regardless of the month. But once June rolled around, I'd be sure I had some plugs and minnow imitations in that box, too.

I'm not sure about the reasons for the shift. Do pike wise up? On their Canadian trip last year my friends Ray and Stan caught the same 21-pounder two days in a row. But that fish had never seen a lure. What of pike that get fished and not caught? In other words, does pike behavior change with fishing pressure? Specifically, fishing pressure with spinners. Well, there's a research project on it. I'm not kidding.

*This high-flying pike tries to throw a plug.*

A 1969 study conducted in the Netherlands analyzed fishing pressure in a pond containing 57 pike that had never before been fished. Five anglers alternated between spinners and bait, with the methods equally effective on the first day. On the following two days only 2 of these 57 "experienced" fish were recaptured with a spinner. In contrast, some 37 of these fish were recaptured by bait, roughly the same success rate that bait fishermen maintained with inexperienced pike. The researchers concluded the following: "Catchability with spinner fishing decreased to very low levels after about half of the population had been caught in this way. Catchability to live bait fishing remained unaffected both by intensive spinner and live bait fishing." The researchers noted that a pike need not be landed to gain experience, that it could do so from simply being hooked—or perhaps from witnessing other pike getting hooked, struggling, and then being whisked into the great blue beyond. There's no evidence on this last point, but I have to wonder whether these sorts of scenes leave the witnesses suspicious.

So do pike wise up about spinners? Those pike sure did. What about pike in the wild? My guess is that the results would be less conclusive. Do pike that get fished be-

come more wary or suspicious of certain flashy imitations? More likely. Do more realistic imitations of a vulnerable forage help in these situations? Perhaps.

Plugs have been around since the turn of the century. Few, if any, began their existence as pike lures, although from the start wood caught northerns. In Dixie Carroll's
1920 survey, plugs accounted for 14 of 50 pike, of which 6 fell to a red and white
plug, presumably a Bass Oreno, the most common bass plug at the time.

   Certain plugs developed reputations as pike catchers, even if they were designed
and promoted for other species. The Pikie Minnow is a good example. In the 1941
*Field & Stream* fishing contest—*the* fishing contest of its day—the Pikie Minnow accounted for 6 of the top 10 northerns.

   The Pikie Minnow was also my uncle Frank's favorite pike plug, and it stood out
from others in the tackle box, occupying its own compartment, the way a stable's best
horse gets his own stall. Tooth marks freckled the olive-barred flanks, proof of this
plug's prowess. Since my uncle and I didn't have a boat, we didn't catch many pike.
But the fishing was exciting, and I can remember standing on shores casting those
scarred old plugs, braced for a toothy maw to appear any minute.

## GOOD WOOD

These days, anglers use four types of plugs to cover most pike-fishing situations: float-
ing/diving (crankbaits), sinking, neutral-density jerkbaits, and floating. It doesn't
matter which brands or models you use in each category, though we all have our
preferences.

   My favorite crankbait is the Cotton Cordell Rattlin' Shad. I have one that I've used
for 10 years now, and it's got more scratches than an Elvis 45. I save it for special occasions. About one in three of these plugs runs properly when you take it out of the
box. You can adjust them by fooling with the lip, but don't overdo it. They come in all
shades. I favor three to the exclusion of others: chrome (my 10-year-old); gray and
white, with an orange belly; and chartreuse. These plugs run about 8 feet on a cast
with 6-pound test. Shad Raps make good choices, too. Bagley makes a nice series of
shad-shaped crankbaits, and they offer a bigger profile than the Shad Rap and Rattlin'
Shad. I usually end up casting the Bass'n Shad, but there's a magnum model, too.

   Many of these crankbaits have rattles in them, but I'm never sure whether they're
successful because of the rattle or in spite of it. Rattletraps are often touted as great
pike lures. An angler once explained that he used them with great success in a shallow, weedy bay just down the road from his store. They were the only lure he used for
northerns. I was headed out fishing there, so I grabbed a handful of traps off the plug

*Shallow-running plugs are good choices during late spring and early summer.*

rack, took 'em like a pike sucking in a slow-trolled chub. This fellow was also a guide and apparently quite unimpressed with the fact that I was working on a pike book.

"Doesn't the Rattletrap get hung up in the weeds?" I asked.

"Just keep the rod tip up high and reel quickly."

"But the weeds are almost up to the top of the water."

"You know," he said, "I can tell just from the way you're talking that there's a lot I can show you."

As it turned out, the Rattletraps didn't catch me any pike that day, nor did any other lures for that matter, leaving my friend Marcel Rocheleau to conclude that "there probably is a lot he can show you." In the end Rattletraps may have a place in your tackle box even if they come in like a tube full of BBs. Unlike the counterintuitive crankbait, which digs deeper the faster you retrieve it, Rattletraps are lipless and sink of their own accord and, as a result, offer more precise control over depth. You can even jig them.

At times I turn to the sinking Rapala in open water. It makes a good deep-water jerkbait, with blue and silver a top choice in open water, Fire Tiger near weeds. As with a Rattletrap, you can control the depth of a sinking Rapala by counting it down to the desired depth before retrieving.

I sometimes use either the chartreuse and silver Fat Rap or white Cotton Cordell Big-O in shallow water of 5 feet or so, though in general I prefer the slim-shaped Rebels and Rapalas. The Floating Rapala, probably the most effective shallow-running plug for pike, comes in all sizes, shapes, and colors. I generally carry silver and black, gold and black, chartreuse, orange, and Fire Tiger. Rapalas will pick up spring pike and are great choices for aggressive fish during the late spring and early summer, and again in fall, as are jerkbaits such as Rattlin' Rogues, which let you fish a little deeper (depending on the model) than the Rapalas. Moreover, jerkbaits enjoy a neutral density, so you can hold them at a desired depth.

By all means, vary your retrieves. Like most anglers, I usually start out with a slow, steady retrieve, except when fishing Rattletraps, which seem to perform best when retrieved briskly. Sometimes I try reeling as soon as the plug hits the water (to get it down and working), slow things down midway through the retrieve, and then speed up near the boat. If I see a pike following, I generally slow down the plug—but I also try to shift the plug's direction so that it moves parallel to the boat. Some anglers believe that following pike lose sight of the lure (their long snout may obstruct their vision), and that this maneuver brings the target right back in view.

My own experience has been that both the stop-and-go and erratic retrieves seem effective during late spring–early summer. I'm not sure why; it may be related to the increasing weed growth, which permits better ambushing. With panfish or baitfish in a post spawn, weakened state, pike may be on the lookout for a forage fish in trouble. I also think plugs increase your chances of hooking a bigger fish, though again I can point to no persuasive reason why. Perhaps a plug offers pike the closest thing to a big forage in trouble. In a sense a crankbait does "swim" like a perch or small walleye or bass hooked on a line, and those hooked fish often induce strikes from bigger northerns.

## WRIGGLES

Plugs weren't the first minnow imitations. Spinners and spoons dressed with pork rinds have been in use since the mid–19th century. These slivers of pickled pork, usually rigged on a spoon or spinner, were not only twitched but also skittered, skipped, skimmed, and skedaddled through pike cover. They seemed the perfect imitation of a frightened baitfish. Skittering was particularly popular with the chain pickerel crowd in New England, and with early northern pike anglers prowling the lagoons and bays of the Great Lakes.

As a kid, I never understood the appeal of pork. I can remember my uncle telling me how good it worked, but the only pork rinds I saw were dried-up curls stuck to the bottom of his tackle box. I had a change of heart after a day of fishing on a shallow, weedy lake with one of my dad's friends, a burly, good-natured fellow named Red Williams.

Fishing with bobbers and minnows, we caught a couple of small pike, but lost more than we hooked in the weeds and quickly ran out of minnows. I tried Dardevles, but the garden was pretty thick. Red opened his tackle box. "Try this Silver Minnow and put a piece of pork rind on the back of it," he said. "It's a good lure in weeds."

He was right. I hooked a pike or, to be honest, the pike hooked itself, snapping at the lure near the boat. It was only 4 pounds or so, but that's a big fish when you're 13 and fishing with an adult you don't know very well. The pike gave me a chance to affect a nonchalant air, the way you were supposed to with pike. Inside, of course, it was circus time in the big tent.

As a result, I developed confidence in the Silver Minnow and pork rind, and the combo responded by teaching me to experiment with retrieves. I'd hook pike with a steady retrieve, the spoon rocking lazily, the pork jitterbugging off the back. But I'd hook other fish, ones that had ignored the vanilla retrieve, by identifying a pike hangout and then retrieving steadily until the lure reached the target area, at which point I'd let it fall for a couple of feet before twitching it to life and *bang!*

There are definitely times when pike in weeds want hardware. The Mepps Cyclops and twister tail can be a good choice in deeper water, but I usually start with the Silver Minnow, going with Fire Tiger over silver in stained water. The Rapala spoon gives much the same sort of action, and if anything seems to work better without a trailer, whereas the Silver Minnow needs to fly a flag, in my opinion. A plastic worm or four-tail twister is less trouble than the pork, if a hair less effective.

Nearly 10 years after I fell for the supple wiggle of a pork rind, I met a bait with even wilder moves. I'd just graduated from college and was relaxing in the fertile, rolling Champlain Valley of Vermont. My friend Ralph Ringer phoned and invited me to fish with him in Little Otter Creek, right where it entered Lake Champlain. "The water's up in the weeds," he explained. "Bass and pike should be biting." Why not? On the way I stopped at the local bait store to pick up a Silver Minnow and some pork rind. "Fresh out of both," the guy said. "Sorry."

My college roommate Irwin Grossman, in the middle of his own postgraduation sojourn, joined us. It was a sunny day, wind from the south, water rippling back into the marshes. Too much of a chop for the Hula Poppers we'd been hoping to use. Ralph had the one Silver Minnow spoon and, good host that he was, gave it to Irwin, who promptly caught a 4-pound pike with it. I looked through my meager tackle box then noticed Irwin's pike, belly-up on the stringer.

"Mind if I do some surgery on your fish, Irwin?"

"Better him than me." Which I took as a yes and carved a pair of pennant-shaped strips of meat off the belly. I'd seen Uncle Frank perform this operation on perch, and my favorite fishing writer, H. G. Tapply, had written about using strip baits for northerns in the "Sportsman's Notebook" series in *Field & Stream.* As Tap suggested, I left the strip an inch wide at one end and then trimmed it to a taper at the other. I lobbed the slab of flesh out to the nearest weeds. It hit with a meaty *splat.*

"Sounds like pike food, anyway," Irwin said.

We eased into a tiny cove that had some marshy spikes poking through the surface. I flopped out the bait, and it vanished in a swirl.

"Look at that," I announced. I dropped the rod, flipped the bail, and the line fell off in coils like a Slinky.

The run stopped, the line tightened and twitched, and I struck hard. A short-lined northern in heavy cover is a fish to be wrestled aboard, and I made no exception for this 6-pounder. Ralph jabbed a boat net beneath the fish and lifted the whole mess on board, which is when the real fight started, with the pike flapping and gear, beer, and swamp muck flying around the boat.

We spent quite a bit of time exploring the marsh that June and the next one, too, enough time to qualify us as competent pike belly anglers. The trick was to respond immediately to the take, which was not as easy as it sounds. The bait would hit the water and curl and straighten. You'd give it a twitch and it would swim. Sometimes you'd see the wake of an ambushing fish, then a fat swirl, at which point you had to flip the

*Pike belly stripbaits. Note the two-tone effect.*

bail immediately to give the fish some slack so it could run. You had to let the feeding continue for a moment or you'd just pull the meat out of the pike's mouth. But I didn't mind the wait, came to enjoy the clandestine connection, enhanced somehow by the ferocity of any creature that so lustily ingests a piece of itself. Those northerns would wait on the edge of the weeds and swallow strips of their own bellies as easily you or I might devour a slice of pizza.

There are times in life when you don't take things very seriously, even fishing. But then you'll go and witness something that gets your attention and you can't get it out of your head. On calm mornings at the junction of Little Otter and East Creeks, where the water was clear and the bottom was dark, we'd sometimes be able to see the pike actually chomp down on the flesh. The white strip would disappear and then reappear as two specks of white bouncing along the bottom in a convulsive sacrificial dance.


## THE JOY OF CANNIBALISM

Do pike know what they are eating when they tear into a strip of their flesh? For years I thought they must, then I was convinced they didn't. These days, I'm not so sure.

Do big pike select for juvenile pike? There's no evidence of that sort of behavior for any pike forage. Big pike do eat small pike whenever the opportunity arises, however. After all, juvenile pike is one meal available in every pike lake. And, in June, pike of all sizes share habitat.

My friend Ray Coppinger loves to tell about the following pike-eating-pike incident that took place far north in Canada. "I have this 8- or 9-pounder in the boat, and he's swallowed my Cleo. Stan and I have a method for removing the hook. He's got strong fingers, so he gets his gloves on and pries open the jaws, and then I can get my needle-nose pliers in there and free the lure. The pike often take the lure deeply, and sometimes you have to back it out through the gills and clip the line. It's a two-man job if you want to save the fish and your fingers.

"I've got this fish on board, pinned against the side so it won't injure itself or me. Stan reels in his line so he can help, and he hooks a small pike—about 20 inches— right at the boat. This fish swallows the lure, too.

"Stan says, 'I'll just let him sit there so we can do your pike.' He flips his bail, and lets the pike drop down to the bottom.

"Well, anybody who thinks pike can't jump should have been in the boat with us. We're working on my pike and all of a sudden Stan's little pike comes flying out of that water two, three times. I'm talking Olympic quality. The last time, it nearly jumps over the bow.

"Stan says, 'Maybe there's a big pike down there.' But he's busy getting his little pike off the line. We've released mine, so I toss out my Cleo and nail an 18-pounder right beneath the boat. That's when we realized how much big pike must love little pike."

They do, no question. How that cannibalism actually transpires is another question. Do pike suddenly turn on one another in the same weedbed? Do attacked pike fight back? Like virtually everything else about pike behavior, there's a study on it.

A 1982 experiment (see *Pike: Biology and Exploitation,* John F. Craig, editor) conducted in the Netherlands addressed these questions. Researchers stocked a 5.5-by-1.2-by-.8 meter aquarium (equipped with artificial weeds) with 16 pike, 4 of which were 16 inches, 10 of which were 10 inches, and 2 of which were 6 inches. (The lengths are approximate, converted from centimeters.) They fed them bream periodically. The results are worth quoting in full:

After introduction all pike swam vigorously through the aquarium without interaction. The next morning 14 resided within the vegetation, with two larger pike in the open area. Ten days after introduction, four 10-inch pike had been eaten; the two six-inch pike escaped predation. Except when foraging the pike did not interact [talk about your understatement!]. Pike positioned themselves parallel to one another. If the longitudinal body axes of pike that encountered one another were perpendicular, the smaller pike arched the body, opened the mouth slightly and protruded the mouth bottom and gills. This threatening posture effectively warded off further approaches. Up to the beginning of May no further losses occurred.

That changed. Here's how:

4 May 1982. Two pike of ten inches were introduced consecutively. Upon introduction both remained stationary, pressed their fins against the body, and moved away from the vegetation and the pike concentration. Within one–two minutes they were swiftly approached from behind by one of the larger pike (the "larger" pike are 16 inches). The larger pike nosed the smaller one in the vicinity of the anal fin. On both occasions the smaller pike turned, was grasped immediately, and was swallowed.

6 May 1982. Four hundred pike fingerlings of two inches did not move upon introduction, sank to the bottom like 'wooden debris' (Franklin and Smith, 1963) and spread over the unvegetated bottom. At first no reaction was observed. However, all fingerlings were eaten overnight. [Finger food?]

***Pike contend with cannibalism even upon reaching adulthood (side by side pictures), as these two pictures of the same fish indicate. Stan Warner.***

12 May 1982. Two pike of 14 inches were removed from the aquarium, kept in isolation in complete darkness for 24 hours and reintroduced in bright light. Initially they acted identically to the 10 inch pike mentioned above. However, after being touched by the larger (16 inch) pike, both turned very fast, instantaneously adopting the threat posture, whereupon the attacker withdrew.

The researchers conclude that "the difference in vulnerability to cannibalism between pike foreign to the aquarium population and the reintroduced members of the population suggests that members of an aggregation may recognize one another."

Interesting. If you buy it, the conclusion begins to explain why it may be in a pike's best interest to remain in one area rather than venture into a new weedbed where all the pike are strangers. And why bigger pike are more inclined to move about. The nosing behavior is interesting. Does it indicate a hesitancy, that of a larger approaching pike trying to recognize this creature? Or is the maneuver a foraging strategy that leaves the smaller fish vulnerable by touching an area of sensitivity so it turns into the waiting pike's open mouth? (As Ray and Stan have shown me, if you want to stimulate a pike on its release, simply squeeze it behind the anal fin and it will zoom off).

If the goal is to control a long, dangerous forage (such as another pike of approximately the same size), then nosing the anal fin would seem a safer strategy than grabbing the prey in the middle of its body. If nothing else, this study certainly reveals why the "figure eight" works—why, in other words, reversing the direction of a lure or fly once it has been nosed by a following pike at the boat often results in a strike. It's also interesting that the reintroduced pike respond with an act of aggression rather than of submission. They know they might get eaten, in other words—much as Stan's pike did when it jumped over the boat. We often see scars on large pike and assume them to be caused by outboard engines. Couldn't those long scars be the result of a particularly active dinner? Or a truly giant pike? Finally, it's tempting, after this study, to say that pike don't eat those from their own neighborhood, but I doubt it.

Many gamefish feed on the fingerlings of their species, but few can match the pike when it comes to gusto for the feast. In the above study, 16-inch pike tried to eat 14-inch pike. Twelve pike (6 to 16 inches long) ate 400 1½- to 2-inch pike. All of them. Overnight. Pike may not select for smaller pike, but this much is for certain: They eat them every chance they get.

So. When a slice of pike belly comes wriggling into view, the pike might not know what it is when it starts the attack, but it must know that it has part of itself when it eats the slice. In light of the nosing behavior in the above study, the smell and slime must indicate a pike taste that means, at the very least, come and get it.

## MEAT SUBSTITUTES

As noted above, fishing strips are generally cut from the pike's belly and lower flank, so that they retain a sort of two-toned appearance. Narrow, finely tapered, 6-inch strips afford the sexiest wiggles, and a little chewing sometimes improves the action, though you should let the pike do that. I generally rig a weedless 1/0 or 2/0 hook and flip it around with a medium-action spinning rod. Deeper than 10 feet, and it works best on a jighead.

The action of these "baits" is quite remarkable, and you should watch one in the water and improvise. My preference is for the erratic, with stops and starts and plenty of settling time through the depths. Pike strikes will often be surprisingly tentative, as if they nose it before grabbing it.

Pike bellies do require the sacrifice of a small pike, even if they involve an inedible portion of that fish. We live in a time of substitutes, though, and this is one bait that can be imitated—and to be honest I'm at a point where I enjoy the imitating part of fishing. For that reason, I've added the pike-colored Pikie Minnow to my starting lineup. The plug seems a little on the drab side, so I press a thumbnail-sized spot of prism tape to its midsection to give the pike something to aim at. Cabela's sells a baby northern pike plug for a fair amount of money, but I'm a sucker, so I have a couple of them, too. Since young pike have vertical bars during the first couple of years of life and thereafter take on the coloration of adults, I use the Pikie Minnows for the former, the Cabela's plug for the latter. I am ready for all age groups.

Do these imitations work better than bright colors or basic shiner patterns? It certainly would be nice if they did, but they don't. I just like using them, that's all. Perhaps it's the fly fisher in me, but I enjoy most the lures that actually imitate something the fish likes to eat; it's the difference, I suppose, between baiting and fooling. Which is a small point, I know, or even no point, depending on how you look at it. At any rate, it gives me some satisfaction.

The limitations of a plug emerge in its woodenness, so to speak, in its texture or lack thereof. A plug simply has no moves, quite in contrast to strip baits, pork rinds, and such, which are nothing but moves. The actual working of strip baits—twitching them through the shallows, probing weedy nooks—is something I've always enjoyed. Fly fishers, of course, go through entire days in this fashion. For others, the closest substitute borrows from the world of plastics and the soft jerkbaits marketed for largemouth fishermen. These artificials don't have the improvisational wriggles and twitches of a pike belly or pork rind, but they offer an intriguing substitute—soft-textured, weightless action that depends entirely on how they are presented and manipulated. What more could you want?

Slug-Gos are probably the most common. Berkley Power Slugs are quite popular, too, though their scent seems largely wasted on pike. Bass Assassins can be good choices, as can Guido's Scattershads. Mann's Shadow provides a good-looking minnow. In my opinion Culprit Jerkworms are the best. They not only glide and slide, but they have impregnated sparkles and a fish shape.

These jerkbaits work when other lures don't, and that counts for a lot in my boat. With the hook hidden, they dip deep into cover, and at times that's where the pike are—even on remote lakes. Once, several summers ago, I was fishing a Canadian reservoir with Ray and Stan. We'd had excellent fishing the evening we arrived, but were chased off the reservoir by a fierce storm. Sharp northwest winds and bright blue skies greeted us the next morning.

"I love this," said Stan. "We drive eight hours to fish the mother of all cold fronts." The active pike from the evening before were nowhere to be found. We worked shorelines, trying plugs, spinners, and spoons with no luck. One pike finally followed a soft jerkbait (it was a Guido's Scattershad), but it wouldn't take. I hacked and carved and trimmed the Scattershad (it's the old strip-bait fisherman in me) so that it was slender and had a bit more action. I laid that bait in a small hole in the driftwood, a pike nailed it, and I drove the hooks into our first decent fish of the day.

At its best close to cover, the jerkbait should be fished slowly with "walk-the-dog" twitches. That Canadian trip was my first experience with jerkbaits and pike, and as the sun warmed the reservoir shoreline, the northerns became quicker to leave their hideouts, often taking the bait as it settled to the bottom. Once, I made a cast and turned to close my tackle box. When I looked back up, my line was on the opposite side of the boat.

Stan observed that he thought I had a bite. I thanked him for his insight and set the hook into a nice beaver dam. The pike had run with the "minnow" just as it might with a live bait. In the years since I generally drop the rod tip, count to three, and set the hook as hard as possible. And pay attention as the jerkbait settles to the bottom.

I prefer 5/0 or 6/0 hooks so that the point can dig into the fish. You can rig the bait Texas-style, which leaves it weedless, but do keep the point of the hook close to the skin of the bait. Hooking fish is always an issue with soft jerkbaits, and you don't want the hook point to fight its way through much plastic before it bites into fish.

Some of these plastics come with weights, but in my opinion the weight of the hook and wire leader is plenty. Weight hinders performance, because the bait's action comes in the glide and slide, from literally the absence of weight. If the fish are down so deep that you need weight, you're much better off with a plastic worm, twister, or shad and jighead.

You can control the depth quite easily. Twitch the bait, pause, then resume the retrieve. The jerkbait is working all the time, and it gives you the sense that the pike are responding not only to the jerkbait's inherent appeal but to how you fish it, as well. In other words, you get to imitate prey behavior with jerkbaits. You can really lose yourself in the angling.

Do the northerns rip them up? Sometimes they do, and sometimes on the first strike. But you can also go quite awhile without putting on a fresh bait. On the Canadian trip I'd fished the same Guido's Scattershad all morning, taking at least 10 or 12 fish on it, before I lost it in the beaver dam. It was getting chewed up. But in an odd way—wet-fly or nymph fishermen will know what I mean here—the more it was chewed, the better it got. True, the morning was warming and the fish were getting more active. Let me put it this way: A few ragged edges didn't hurt it one bit.

*A soft jerkbait is a deadly bait when pike are sluggish and holding tight to cover.*

Jerkbaits come in some wild colors, and it makes sense to match the color to the water stain. I return used baits not to their original package but to gallon freezer bags, in one of which I put all chartreuse and yellow plastics (including twister tails and worms), and in another of which I put all orange and gold. I keep a third as my sack of many colors. The idea is less to get biblical than to permit these colors to bleed into one another so that, for instance, clear sparkled jerkworms remain translucent but also pick up a sort of a hue, be it orange, chartreuse, yellow, or a combination thereof. In the end the plastics in the sack of many colors take on a palomino coloring, a mottled appearance that leaves them looking for all the world like little pike.

On mild mornings in early June, when the water is clear and flooding the shore-line weeds, when the North Country is blooming into fertility, these mottled oddball jerkbaits feel like the thing to use. They remind me of a time a generation ago when I entered the Little Otter Creek marsh indifferently and casually, encountered the ferocity of a pike's shallow-water world, and left a committed (committable?) pike fisherman.

The jerkbaits may not wiggle like a belly strip, but they retain the shape and tex-ture and behavior of small pike. Remember that in the study, the 400 fingerlings "did not move upon introduction, sank to the bottom like 'wooden debris.' " What better imitation of this behavior than the gliding descent of a soft jerkbait?

Such a fine point may well be lost on the pike, ultimate opportunists that they are. But it's not lost on me.

# 8

# Top Water

My friend Chris Loftus is a serious fisherman. He spends the month of June in his canoe, casting his way around the shallow bass ponds and lakes just inland from Lake Ontario. He knows the ponds so well he can predict the species and size of the fish that will strike a plug before it hits the water. For 23 years old, he's an accomplished angler. He releases all his fish, bass and northerns. "They're really more like my pets," he told me.

When I explained that I was writing a book on pike, he invited me along. "I know this one pond with some good-sized northerns," he said. "And you can get them on the surface this time of year. You should see them try to catch a Zara Spook. Or a buzzbait."

The next morning found us paddling up the outlet to a pond, scrunching beneath oak branches and whooshing through thick undergrowth. Through some thick mosquitoes, too. At times we had to get out and carry the canoe over the exposed streambed. Then we emerged from the understory to the open water, flushing a pair of squealing wood ducks into the soft June air. We put the paddles to work in the quiet water.

"The bay just beyond that weedline is a good spot for northerns," Chris said. "It's got a sharp drop-off. They come up there in the morning. Get ready."

We glided up to the weedline, and Chris positioned the canoe next to an opening in the reeds that formed an alley into the pike bay. I winged out a Zara Spook and a bloom of monofilament appeared on my baitcaster.

I glanced at the plug rocking gently, rings subsiding, and turned my attention to the tangle, yanking at the backlash. Then I looked back up at the plug, still as a statue, pulled the last snarl free, and began reeling the excess line back onto the spool. I must have inadvertently twitched the plug, because it began to "walk." The pond was so calm that when a tuft of grass shivered 10 yards from the plug, we both saw it. I looked back at the reel and saw that I had a few yards yet to go. Almost there.

"We've got company," Chris said.

Moments later a green and black figure crashed across the surface. The water flew, I set the hook, and the Zara Spook zipped back at us. *Boink.* It bounced off the side of the canoe.

"I know, I know," I said. "Too quick. Too much coffee."

"This should be quite a book."

## SURFACE CONVERSIONS

The Puritans did away with bear baiting, legend has it, not because it was cruel to the bear, but because it was so much fun to watch. It's a good thing they never caught on to top-water pike fishing.

Anglers in North America quickly became aware of the fun of top-water pike, as the following 1869 rendition of surface fishing indicates. As he noted in *Fishing in American Waters,* Genio Scott preferred

> a Buel's or McCarg's spoon, mounted with red ibis feather, and white feathers or hair for the under side of the spoon . . . [you] stand near the bow of your punt, and skitter the lure along the surface of the water, near the margins of the lily-pads, and if you are on Sodus Bay, or tempting the fish from almost any of the bayous of Lake Ontario, you will find cause for surprise that will force you to ejaculate; for it will be questionable which will be most astonished, the novice in the boat or that in the water.

If the pike's role in our fishing community is to provide that moment of adventure in an ordinary trip to the pond next door, the crashing surface strike is its signature entrance. Before there were Discovery Channel crocodiles at wildebeest crossings, there were northern pike in millponds. Sudden as death. If you like watching scary movies, you probably like surface fishing for pike.

My friend Stan Warner is the most dedicated top-water angler I know. "It's gotten so bad that I don't let him drive the boat anymore," moans Ray Coppinger, his fishing buddy.

*Late spring and early summer is a great time to fish surface lures. The strikes can come when you least expect them. This pike has just slammed a buzzbait, nearly at the boat.*

"He'll see a weed or two across the bay, and the next thing I know we're casting poppers and chuggers. We'll spend the next half hour auditioning surface plugs, pike or not."

It's taken me longer, but I'm there. I'd actually rather fish for smaller fish on top than bigger ones on subsurface lures, which is the trade-off you have to make. There's a difference in numbers, too. In all likelihood, for every pike you catch on surface lures, you'll catch three or four on spinnerbaits. You know what? I don't care.

## SURFACE CHOICES

My uncle Frank wasn't big on throwing things out. His tackle box contained a number of lures at least 30 years old, some older than that. One surface plug had a 3-inch wire leader, a scalloped face, and a silver rear spinner. I remember this one in particular because Uncle Frank had identified it as a good one for pike. I used that plug every chance I got, even though I never had a strike on it.

But in retrospect I realize that lure had many of the qualities of the prototypical surface plug for pike: a cylindrical shape, a spinner or prop for some flashy fuss, and a kind of rocking, side-side motion when it was retrieved. Minnow shape, flash, fuss, and motion continue to define the parameters for successful pike surface lures today, just as they did 50 years ago.

Surface crawlers such as Jitterbugs and Crazy Crawlers would not be my first choice in surface plugs, but they make the cut because they are so much fun to use. They emit a melodious *burble-burble-burble* when you retrieve them, to say nothing of leaving a seductive bubble trail in their wake. They always give me the sense that I have one hardworking little plug on my line. A Crazy Crawler lands on the water like a half-grown teal. And their names are at once literal and lyrical, as friend and poet Paul Jenkins noted. The combination of function and music speaks of another time, when fishing lures were made and repaired in garages and basements, when the Creek Chub Bait Company could put on the floor a girl's basketball team, with CCBCO on their uniforms. (Which might say as much about the state of Indiana, where the company was located, as it does about the texture of early-20th-century Americana.) For whatever reason, I have the best luck with these plugs when fishing in water with a lot of obstructions; perhaps the blunt shape and surface burbling fit with the ducklings, muskrats, or frogs that frequent that type of water. Then again, perhaps that doesn't matter.

If you're going to imitate anything, it might as well be a baitfish. The Pop-R makes an effective open-water choice. Chug Bugs, Skitter Pops, and numerous other poppers are probably just as good. Regardless of brand, this type of lure represents the ideal "deep-water" surface lure—namely, a slow-working minnow imitation that attracts a lot of attention with its *cu-chug*. For all-around work, I prefer the propellered, minnow-shaped plugs. Smithwick's Devil's Horse is an old standard that works very well, although in recent years I have come to use the Dying Flutter, which resembles the Devil's Horse but has longer propellers and a shorter, more tapered body. I can't imagine the pike taking one and not the other, however.

These stickbait plugs kick up a fuss and can be retrieved in a variety of ways. You're restricted to the *chug* with the Pop-R, which is quite loud and, I suppose, can be heard at a greater distance. But the only elements of the retrieve you can vary are how hard to pop and how long to wait between pops. You can employ a quick series of lighter *blub, blub, blubs,* but this has never been an effective pike retrieve for me.

Propellers give a resonant *blip* when you twitch them, and you can adjust the noise during the presentation. Retrieve it in sharp *blips* with pauses between; light twitches with little noise—just enough to get the propellers spinning (hence the name *Dying Flutter,* I suppose); or maintain a steady retrieve with a brief pause halfway back to the boat. These are all pike-catching retrieves and the trick is to figure out which most successfully accommodates the northerns' mood at the moment.

In a steady retrieve the plug actually functions as a buzzbait, which can be an absolute riot to fish. The standard buzzbait, with a revolving wing, is at its best around open-water structure such as brush piles or tree branches or even copses of emergent plants. It's fun to rip buzzbaits through the water, but my own experience has been that they should be retrieved at a deliberate pace. You don't want the lure to *buzz* as much as *wip-wop-wip-wop.* Sometimes it pays to vary the speed of buzzbaits by casting beyond the target and cranking it right along, slowing it down by the wood or brush, then speeding up as it draws away. Pike-fishing expert Jack Penny describes the classic surface presentation in a recent edition of *Waterwolf* (the delightful and

*Minnow-shaped propeller plugs like this Devil's Horse are a good starting point for topwater. Note hard monofilament leader.*

useful publication of Pikemasters): "Throw one of those [in-line] buzzbaits and let it sit for a few seconds. Then give it a big rip, followed by a slow retrieve, twitching it every so often. The rip is to attract their attention and the slow retrieve is for triggering them."

The knock against buzzbaits is that pike miss them more than they hit them. In recent years I've found myself moving away from the winged buzzbaits and relying more on in-line versions, such as the Sputterbuzz, which has a hard body and a sexy tail, or the spinning blade and tube frog trailer. These in-line buzzbaits can be retrieved more slowly, present a slimmer profile, and offer a lighter touch. They also pick up less vegetation than standard buzzbaits and in general are easier to manipulate.

Finally, no noise can be good noise when the surface world is cemetery still. The Zara Spook, as my friend Chris Loftus indicated, is not at all a bad choice when used, in his words, "by a responsible adult." Floating Rapalas, twitched on top, can be terrific. But the Spook has that "I'm-a-disoriented-minnow-where-the-hell-am-I-going?" thing working. In a sense it is an exaggeration of the rocking motion of Uncle Frank's old rear-paddle pike plug, and the northerns absolutely whack it. The irony is that I miss more northerns on the Spook than on the buzzbait; perhaps the erratic movement is like a ninth-inning knuckleball after eight innings of heat.

## TOP-WATER TACTICS

You'll hear of plugs pulling fish off the bottom in 15 feet of water, but the water better be clear and glassy with good numbers of schooling shad or minnows. Depths of 10 feet and under offer the best chance at a surface strike. Even then, in water as shallow as 5 feet pike will often ignore surface lures. Surface-oriented pike do associate with obstructions of one kind or another, but you won't find them back in the jungle like a largemouth. Since pike tend to ambush into open water, weedless surface lures are unnecessary.

Pike seem most inclined to come to the surface when the water is in the high 50s and low 60s and the light is diffused. Mornings and evenings make the best times, though quiet, cloudy afternoons, with the stillness before the storm hanging in the air, can bring the best surface fishing of all. Sunlight and wind, on the other hand, discourage surface feeding. The wave action not only refracts the light and blurs the image of the target, it keeps the target itself bouncing around and prevents the pike from

*This northern took a plastic frog, which was intended to prove a point that a northern wouldn't take such a bait. Note: flat calm conditions; note also, wire leader, just in case. Stan Warner.*

drawing aim. Northerns have to make hits on first tries, or at least have a good chance at success, or they begin losing the fight to build more energy than they expend. So they avoid feeding in surface turbulence, when they can.

Work the small coves and points formed by false shores of emergent vegetation. On flows, rivers, and smaller lakes the quiet water beneath overhanging branches and bushes can be good, too. If you don't get a hit probing the shoreline, a long cast parallel to the shore with a propeller minnow or buzzbait can sometimes provoke a strike. I suppose it's the surface angler's version of trolling.

In general, I fish surface lures as slowly as my nerves permit. Any lure benefits from a 15-second wait before you start the retrieve. If you can wait a little longer, so much the better. And I probably use lighter lines than most anglers, preferring 10-pound, with 17-pound in the thick cover.

As for leaders, I make my own, with 30-pound hard (saltwater) mono or nylon-coated bluefish wire that comes in a tippet spool. Whatever the choice, I tie it to a swivel on one end and a snap on the other. This arrangement holds up longer than you'd think, and it doesn't inhibit the action of the plugs. Some lures can take a regular wire leader and still keep their action—Crazy Crawlers, Jitterbugs, and Devil's Horses, to name a few. But for the most part you're better off with as little weight as possible.

Of course, this fussing around doesn't preclude some snot-nosed kid catching a pike the size of a beagle on a plastic floater he fished out of the 25-cent bin. In general, pike are no more selective (in the imitative sense) about surface baits than about subsurface lures. But they do respond to certain triggers. Underwater preferences seem to fall into categories of action and color; top-water preferences often organize around speed of retrieve, shape of the bait, and the type or amount of disturbance the lure makes. Interestingly, pike in one part of a bay can be surface minded and those in another part absolutely indifferent to things pattering across the ceiling.

Several years ago Stan Warner and I were fishing a lake on the Canadian border. A midday June sun burned through the haze. The water lay still beneath what was to become the afternoon's spongelike humidity. I began fishing with streamers on my fly rod, Stan with a variety of top-water plugs on his spinning tackle. We floated around on a shallow reef, and I came close to diving in for a dip. We worked our way into one of the bays, where intermittent pond weeds began showing up.

"What do you think?" I asked.

"Looks pretty shallow," Stan said. But he was content because we were definitely in top-water territory. He caught a small pike on a Chug Bug, on his first cast, then another two casts later. I'd never get him out of there.

I clipped on a hair bug with long, trailing saddle hackles, and that drew one half-hearted swirl. Meanwhile Stan switched to a buzzbait and took several pike in the 25- to 26-inch range, at which point I was relieved that we'd left the tent in the van. I put on my in-line buzzbait tube frog and started catching northerns, too.

These pike were in 5 feet of water, but less for the shallow depth than for the weed cover. The weeds thickened once you hit the 4-foot line, thinned at 7 feet. In between the pike swarmed on the hunt, even as the afternoon sun drove the air temperature through the 80s. We probably caught 50 pike between 1 and 4 P.M. The biggest might have made 7 pounds, but they gave us more action than an attic full of gray squirrels.

That evening we returned to the offshore edge of the reef in hopes of some bigger fish. And we did catch some nice northerns, several of which reached 10 pounds. Closer to shore the pike had been jumping over one another to grab those infernal buzzbaits that blathered their way over the tops of the weeds. But here on the outside edge they wouldn't come to the top, even though the water was only several feet deeper. Instead they all took white spinnerbaits. It was an altogether instructive day of fishing.

For now it is worth noting that surface fishing for pike probably includes more nuance than we recognize, so entranced are we by their slashing strikes. The shallow fish that fed on top had some sort of advantage in the particular weed density they had selected, and they were certainly exercising it. They wanted a fast-paced lure, and they wanted some burble with it. Without it, the catch dropped off. Stan and I had enough time and fish so we could experiment. Color meant nothing; shape meant nothing. It was all in the buzz.

*Buzzbaits can be excellent pike lures when retrieved just a bit slower than you would for bass.*

In other words, the pike assumed a selectivity different from other gamefish, although not necessarily different from other predators. They had to be selective regarding where they could hunt, which cover they could use, and which prey they could take. And there were some size restrictions. Bigger pike simply couldn't feed in the shallow water, even though the forage must have been in there, given the concentration of active fish. The bigger pike remained outside, in the 7- to 12-foot range, but they didn't take any top-water lures, and with Stan in the boat you never come away worrying that you didn't give your surface plugs a true test. Perhaps the bigger pike couldn't risk investing all that energy in an unsuccessful top-water strike in 68-degree water. Perhaps they couldn't get close enough; or perhaps the ripples prevented them from getting a good look at the target—in the way that a three-point shooter in basketball likes to get a good look at the basket before taking a shot with the game on the line.

Those bigger pike on the outside behaved like adult northerns should, except that they wouldn't take a regular spinnerbait retrieve. Instead we caught them by bulging the spinnerbaits just beneath the surface, suggesting that these fish would have taken top-waters had it been glassy. As it was, they snatched up lures inches below the surface. We'd keep our rod tips high and retrieve the spinnerbait slowly and steadily just beneath the surface so that it bulged, then we'd let it drop, then pick up the retrieve again. They'd already be on the line.

## CLOSE-UP

No matter how much you expect a pike strike, its appearance on the surface still comes as a surprise. Like the villain in the scary movie. It's hard to remain composed, and I dread the day that I don't jump a little bit when a pike crashes my plug. Until then, I'll continue to miss pike because I strike too quickly. In my head I know that the trick is to wait until I see the plug disappear, but like most fishing tricks, it is much easier said than done. There's so much commotion; these pike have very poor table manners. My friend Chris Loftus waits until he actually feels the thump of the fish on the line. I've watched him do it, too. Then again, he's 25 years younger than I am, and his nerves have relatively few miles on them.

The truth is pike have trouble catching our surface lures. My friend Ray Coppinger, who has extensively studied canine predation even as he has battled his pike addiction, speculates that pike may actually lose sight of surface baits as they approach them. "This is not at all unusual in the animal world," Ray explains. "Alligators and sharks have the same problem with their long jaws. If they attack straight on, they'll hit you with their nose, so they have to roll or turn to get a better look at you, er, it. The roll or turn may offer an additional advantage in that resulting turbulence may delay the escape of the prey.

"A pike sees a surface lure overhead, sees it struggling along, perhaps stopping occasionally. So that prey is vulnerable, but it's a long way up, 8 feet, let's say. And as the pike sizes things up, it must contend with a three-dimensional problem: The prey is not just across and away, as when it is under water, but it is also on a third axis, the surface, an oddly angled axis, to boot. If the water is still, the pike sees the prey clearly, but bubbles and turbulence cloud its vision as it accelerates during the approach. The pike's eye always wants to focus on the closest objects, the way our eyes focus on the dirt on car windshield rather than the highway ahead. The pike loses sensory contact with the target as it moves and no longer has a prey image. Going faster only makes it worse, but the pike must accelerate to develop the suction necessary for grasping the target. The pike attacks, messily, perhaps missing the lure on the way up, but nailing it on the way down."

As Coppinger notes, in every predator-prey interaction the predator has to decide whether the strike will be successful. If the predator can't catch the prey, it won't try. That decision may be unconscious—like the way we drive a car when we're talking with a passenger. But it really is a matter of cognition, and it influences pike behavior on many levels.

"I believe pike (and most other predators) think like that," says Coppinger. "I remember one time I was fishing in Canada with Stan and Lorna [Coppinger], and I was casting a buzzbait toward shore. A pike came up behind it, but the buzzbait was right up against a log. I couldn't stop the retrieve or the buzzbait would sink into the brush. I had to keep retrieving it, so I hopped it over the logs.

" 'Oh, no,' I said, 'look at that.' And they looked, and I'm glad I had witnesses. The pike saw that my lure was about to go over the log, so it swam around the log and waited for that lure to come over the top—and nailed it when it did. Without a doubt, that fish figured out how to intercept that lure. You can call it what you want; I call it cognition."

Our involvement in the predator-prey drama offers an irresistible doubleness in which we are both manipulator—as Ray was when he decided to keep the lure moving over the log—and victim. We can see the plug clearly, but it is what we don't see that keeps us pinioned in suspense. We surface fish for pike for the same reason that Hitchcock keeps the shower curtain drawn.

If the visceral participation in predator-prey draws us to pike fishing, top water gives our participation a sentiment. Wooden plugs are old pals with painted coats, friendly faces, and familiar little noises. They're more like duck decoys than fishing lures: You might need to touch them up with a little paint now and then, but barring an act of God they're yours for the duration. The nice little Crazy Crawler was swimming home, *wicka-wocka-wicka-wocka,* when along came the big bad pike and CRASH!

It's funny. I hook a trout, salmon, or bass on a top-water lure or fly, and I immediately start worrying that I might lose it. I get there with pike, but before I worry about them getting away, I spend a moment or two enjoying the fact that the tables are turned.

# 9

# Fly Fishing

One May afternoon back in the early 1980s I was fishing with my old friend Buzz LaRose in the Lake Ontario estuary of the Black River. Our trip was a first of sorts in that we were fly fishing for pike. On purpose.

"There's one," Buzz said, and his fly rod forming a 9-foot C as he set the hook.

"Pike?" I asked, hoping.

He tried to pump the fish to the surface but it dove beneath the boat. Buzz plunged his rod in the water so that the tip was below the engine prop, pivoted the rod around the stern, and brought it up on the other side. "Sure acting like one," he said. The fish rolled to the top. Vacant eyes, flaring gills, white spots—northern. He eased it toward the boat. So far, so good—until I touched the pike's tail with the metal rim of the boat net. It was as if the fish were suddenly plugged in; it skittered from the boat side in a tail walk and then dove back down to the weedline.

"Next time maybe try getting the net in the water before he's near the boat," Buzz said out the side of his mouth, his ivory line sawing through the dark water.

When the pike tired, I dug deep and scooped the thrashing fish into the boat. "I need to record this," I said, getting my camera out. "You don't mind, do you?"

Buzz picked up the pike, looked at it. "Hell, no. This fish has a face that makes me look good." He held up the pike and grinned, then slipped it back into the late-spring waters of Dexter Marsh. "I know there's a bigger one in there, what with all these alewives in the river," Buzz continued, working out some line. "Give us a kick out so we get a better drift." I pulled on the starter cord and we were fishing again.

Buzz was a true believer, gone now, dead of a heart attack at 43. Any angler can be a fly fisher in Montana or Idaho, but it takes a true pioneering spirit to wave the long rod in Dexter, New York, where in Buzz's day the debate was not whether there should be a snagging season on chinook salmon but how long it should run. When Nelson Bryant from the *New York Times* came north to report on the new fishery for Great Lakes steelhead, Buzz took him out fly fishing and ended up catching a steelhead—on a stonefly nymph. He handed me Bryant's yellowed article the day we were introduced by a mutual friend, Ted Lehnert. Buzz was a hefty guy, and he had trouble with his knees. He couldn't get up and down the streambanks that well anymore. The article was his way of saying, "I'm for real."

And he was. Buzz caught everything that could swim on a fly rod, and when I said I wanted to catch a pike on a fly, he said meet me at his boat at noon tomorrow.

"Gotta work in the morning?"

"Naw, I've got to get some pike flies tied." The man had his priorities and, when it came to fly fishing, the will of a Himalayan Sherpa. Talk a blue streak, true, but never stop looking for a bigger fish.

Consider what preceded the boat-thrashing pike that Buzzy landed in Dexter Marsh. There were alewives in the river, so we knew there were pike

*Traditionally, few anglers fly fished for pike, but that is changing. Stan Warner.*

around. Walleye fishermen had been catching them incidentally upstream by the town bridge.

We'd been drifting along a 5- to 10-foot weedline. Several smaller pike had followed our streamers to the surface, but they wouldn't take.

"Maybe they want a jigging action," Buzz said. "That's how the walleye fishermen are getting them." He bit down on a split shot and slid it down snug to the eye of the white and silver marabou streamer. He made a cast and shook some line through the guides so that the fly would sink, then began stripping it in, pausing after each strip so that the fly would dart and fall. That's when the pike took.

A few years later Ted Lehnert and I tried fishing some of Buzzy's haunts, and we caught some smallmouths. We didn't catch any northerns until Ted broke out his baitcaster and chartreuse spinnerbait and nailed a 10-pounder alongside an old beaver dam.

"I'm glad Buzz wasn't around to have seen that," Ted said after he released the fish. Ted was right. We would have caught some grief about "dry gulching" that fish, as Buzz called baitcasting, but somehow I don't think I would have minded the ribbing much at all.

Buzz was unique. Twenty years ago not many people fly fished for northerns, particularly in spring when the trout fishing was good.

Only recently, with the flurry of interest in wilderness northerns, have fly fishers devoted much attention to pike. Throughout the 19th and for most of the 20th century fly fishing for pike has enjoyed a sketchy history at best. It rears up now and then, beginning in Walton's time and continuing on and off through the mid–20th century in the United States. Bergman, for instance, gave it a paragraph or two in *Just Fishing*. For the most part fly fishers and northern pike were enemies, much like bird hunters and goshawks.

Fly fishing for northerns began to receive smattering of applause in the early 1960s, as McClane, Brooks, Tapply, and others expanded our ideas of the proper fly-rod quarry. Midwesterner Tom McNally led the cheering. In fact, the McNally Magnum could arguably be called the first modern fly dressed specifically for northerns. With bright colors, hackle body, and long saddle-hackled tail, the fly and its design remain with us today.

Pike articles began appearing in fly-fishing magazines during the 1980s. Most were trip paybacks, focusing on fly-in fishing in northern Canada. Then in 1989 Barry Reynolds and John Berryman wrote *Fly Fishing for Pike*, which offered a comprehensive approach to shallow-water fishing in the western U.S. and Canada. By the 1990s interest in fly fishing for pike had grown to the point that how-to information occasionally appeared in articles in *Fly Fishing Quarterly,* and more

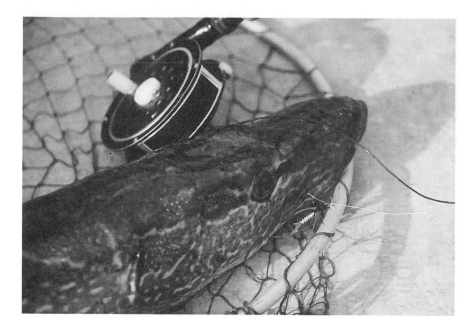

recently in a crisp, new magazine called *Warmwater Fly Fishing,* put out by Abenaki Publishers.

So it was that the fly-fishing community discovered northern pike, though the relationship has some built-in boundaries—and prescriptions. The best fly fishing for northerns occurs during spring, when mayflies hatch and trout feel like the fish you should be pursuing. By the time that most fly fishers get around to thinking about pike, the northerns have drifted off to deeper waters, where they become difficult to catch. As a result, most fly fishers determined to catch pike—and with sufficient means—head north to the Canadian wilderness, where northerns hold in shallow water throughout the season and you can catch a boatload of them.

Like other fly fishers, I have a seasonal rhythm to my angling. I really don't get an opportunity for much in the way of Canadian adventures, either. In recent years, however, I've managed more spring fly-fishing trips for northerns in the northern U.S., particularly in late May and early June. And I haven't been at all disappointed.

## TACKLE AND PRESENTATIONS

I use a 7-weight outfit to fish deep water in the summer, an 8-weight during the spring, and a 9-weight on Canadian adventures. Pike streamers can be good sized, and you also want to be able to set the hook with authority. Northerns don't run that far when hooked, so you don't need fancy reels or 100 yards of backing. If you're hooking 20-pound fish in northern Canada, get a disc drag system; if you're paddling around the fringes of a spring lake, hoping for one that will push 10, a single-action is fine. A bug-tapered, floating line with a 7½-foot leader of 10- to 20-pound test is my choice in shallow water. In 10 feet of water or more I use a Hi-D sinking tip and a 5-foot leader of 10-pound test.

The advantage of the lighter leader is that it allows the fly more action. You do need a shock leader with a fly, and you should make it longer, ironically, than with a lure, because northerns inhale the weightless, slow-moving fly more deeply than they do a heavier metal or wooden plug. I've experimented with various types and have settled on three kinds. The Orvis pike guards work fine, but the twisting of the pike call for frequent rerigging. Ditto for twist-on bluefish wire. The standard 12-inch black wire leader (which many claim is harder for fish to detect than the standard silver wire), available in most tackle stores, works fine. You can also tie your own, which I prefer, with a 2-foot length of 30-pound hard monofilament or with monofilament-coated stainless steel (which I've just begun testing this season; it's used by bluefish anglers who also wish to catch wire-shy stripers. I don't know if it will fray after a single fish, as some such concoctions have in the past). Both of these materials can be fastened with standard knots. Tie a swivel to one end and a cross-lock snap to the other.

Fly-rod strategies parallel those employed with spinning and baitcasting tackle. That is, early spring means slow presentations in shallow water, followed by more aggressive "horizontal" tactics up and down the water column during the late spring and early summer. Next comes the vertical and/or deep, slow horizontal fishing characteristic of summer, followed by a return to aggressive late-spring, early-summer presentations in fall.

Spring and early summer offer the most reliable fly fishing. I've always had the best luck when water temperatures range from 52 to 65 degrees, which is typical for pike fishing in the northern United States and southern Canada from mid-May through mid-June, and in central and northern Canada through summer.

Fly fishing is an excellent choice in the pre-spawn or immediate post-spawn, when fish are spooky, sluggish, and holding in clear, shallow water. Fished on a floating line, big streamers can be worked slowly near cover. By all means, try the streamers without weight first. Let them settle, and twitch them slowly back to the boat.

Since feeding pike almost always look from the shallows toward deeper water, the shallow-water fly fisher does well to fish parallel to the weedlines or cover and make the fly appear like a disoriented panfish or baitfish. That can mean the "slow sink and slow strip" in water of several feet. It can also mean adding a bit of weight—

usually dumbbell eyes (as in a Clouser Minnow) or light split shot—so that you get a more pronounced drop to the fly.

The first person I ever knew who actually caught a pike on a fly was my trout-fishing dad, of all people. He was fly fishing for spring browns in an ice-out lake, wading from shore, and using the slow-sink and slow-strip presentation described above. With sinking line and weighted white marabous, he inadvertently hooked some half a dozen northerns one afternoon.

"Geez, that's something," I said over the phone. I was in college at the time.

"Yeah, I think there were too many weeds there."

Love that pike fishing.

There are, however, several points to take from my dad's northern encounter that cold April afternoon, and the first one is that you need to adjust presentation and gear for various moods and locations of the northern. My dad didn't know it (or maybe he realized it too late), but he had the perfect approach for post-spawn pike: slowly fishing a dropping marabou streamer. Later in spring he would have wanted to try (or avoid!) the steady-strip, strip-and-pause, or strip-and-drop retrieves.

The steady-strip fishes like it sounds, and often works well with active fish in shallow water. I generally start with 4- to 6-inch strips. You can smooth out this retrieve (and vary the speed) by sticking the rod under your arm and using a two-handed strip, although you'll need a stripping basket to execute this retrieve. A bas-

*A sliding plastic worm sinker can be used to sink pike flies. Note hard monofilament leader, hand-tied leader.*

*Pre-spawn finds pike in shallow water, in delta areas of lakes and reservoirs, in places where fly fishing is not only possible, but a good option, as well.*

ket, in general, is not a bad idea, and now that I use one in saltwater fishing, I find it hard not to want it in a boat while freshwater fishing, too.

To fish a strip-and-pause, cast out as far as possible with a sinking-tip line and weightless fly. Let the fly sink to the bottom and retrieve it in fast strips with pauses in between. The strip-and-drop method, which actually produces more fish, is best executed with a floating line and a weighted fly. Swim the fly back in foot-long strips so that it swims, then falls. Pike will often take the fly when it stops. In any case, experiment with retrieves. Given the salience of prey *behavior* in triggering a strike, retrieves play a critical role in the overall pike presentation.

Pike will often follow your fly to the boat. If you have enough line out, maintain your retrieval speed. If your leader is at the rod tip, try stopping the fly, twitching it two or three times, then speeding it up in a direction away from the boat. An even better way is to let the fly drop to the bottom—if the water is deep enough. Each of these tactics work occasionally; much of the time none of them does.

Surface fly rodding for pike is often possible in the late spring, although anytime the fish are shallow and not taking on subsurface patterns, top water is worth trying. The trick is to create a wake and have the hackle feathers or "feet" tripping back to the boat in the fly's wake. Sometimes pike prefer a steady skim that keeps the fly skittering across the surface. Occasionally, pike will go for a pop-and-stop retrieve, but I usually try the wake first. As with any surface bait, nearly all fish misses occur because the angler strikes too quickly. So slow down, feel the fish, and then set the hook by drawing down on the line and simultaneously lifting the rod.

When pike don't strike cast flies, you can take them by drifting with the wind. I'm not sure if the presentation benefits from the fact that you show your fly to a lot of fish, that the long swim fools followers, or that sooner or later a pike runs up against the feathers and snaps at the fly—but it works. You can adjust the depth with split shot and/or sinking lines. Pike on a long line are a blast—they hit hard, and the fight can be quite memorable. But you don't want to cut any corners. They will make you pay.

One June weekend my friend Tony Zappia and I drove over to fish Rich Lake, a pristine patch of blue in the Adirondacks. We met my friend Ralph Ringer and his son Craig at the campsite, just as an evening thunderstorm had washed a week's worth of unseasonable humidity out of the notches and valleys. We were heartened by the news that Ralph and Craig had taken some nice pike on streamers that afternoon.

"Of course, that was before the front went through," Ralph said. "Craig got one that was close to 30 inches. We caught some nice smallmouths too. All on Nine-Threes."

The next morning began bright and sharp, and the wind blew hard out of the northwest. Tony and I were in one canoe, Ralph and Craig in another. The plan was to catch some bass for dinner, then go after pike. Like any campfire plan, it suffers some in the light of day. We worked the shallows with poppers, then hit the drop-offs with crayfish imitations, but the bass were having none of it. By early afternoon we had one 13-inch smallmouth between the two canoes.

"We're going into town to buy some steaks," Ralph called as he and Craig began paddling in to shore.

"Let's just drift the shoreline," Tony said to me. "Maybe we can catch a northern."

I looked through my box for a white marabou and found one, a size 4, 8X long, perfect for drifting. But my wire leaders were buried in a tackle box underneath the cooler. Screw it, I thought, knotting the streamer onto the 6-pound-test leader.

I dropped the streamer over the side, let out the sinking line and we drifted with the wind. My Hi-D sinking tip had the fly down a ways, and I'd added a split shot. Tony had a spoon over the side but was mostly paddling with the wind to keep us straight. We reached the tip of an island, passed over a weedy shoal that jumped up to 10 feet.

*Spring and fall represent the fly fisher's best opportunities because pike are in fairly shallow water.*

"Looks perfect," I said.

Just then my rod twitched, like a perch bite. Tony saw it, too, and when I picked up the rod to set the hook, the line and leader came sliding across the surface. The fly was gone. I never even felt the resistance of a fish.

"Sharp teeth," Tony observed. Just then a swirl the size of a card table showed at the surface some 30 yards behind the canoe. We never saw the fish, and it's probably just as well.

## FLY DESIGN

If the McNally Magnum was the first recognizable pike pattern, old Joe Brooks ties such as the Strawberry Blonde caught some pike, too. Current all-around patterns such as the Clouser Minnow and Lefty's Deceiver make fine pike flies as well.

Reynolds and Berryman include a number of pike patterns in their book; the Bunny Fly, in which Zonker strips are used as a tail and wound as hackle, is particularly productive.

Pike aren't selective for pattern or imitation, but they do have preferences. They definitely like flies that sparkle and shine, and seem inclined to soft materials. That generally means wound marabou or bunny fur, tails made of saddle hackles or Zonker strips, and plenty of Flashabou. Big eyes don't hurt, either.

Part of me wishes it were different. Fly fishermen love to complicate their quarry, and I am here to tell you that I am no slouch in this department. But I've given up, thanks in no small part to my friend Ray Coppinger, who has fashioned a fly-fishing career out of obliterating any notion I might entertain about the selectivity of pike feeding habits. He was at his best one bright summer morning several years ago on a remote lake in northern Quebec.

We were working along a shoreline bordered with logs and driftwood, and the pike were in there in good numbers. On the two or three previous mornings they'd been taking anything we threw at them. We'd cast, let the fly sink. Then strip, strip, pause. Strip, strip—*bang!*

On this morning we'd drifted 100 yards of the shore and had yet to get a hit.

"Maybe the water needs to warm up a bit," said Ray.

"Or maybe they need a color we don't have," I answered.

"Whoop, there we go," Ray said. A pike had taken his fly and was headed for cover. Ray clamped the reel and leaned hard on the 9-weight to keep the fish out of the logs. "Come here and help me land him."

That was strange, as this pike appeared to be no bigger than those he'd been landing by himself all trip. At any rate, I got the net and edged to the back of the boat. There was the pike, a 6-pounder, leering at me, with a big tan fly festooning its snout. I scooped it up before it could dive beneath the boat.

"What pattern is that?" I asked.

"It's one you've never heard of, one of my own creations. I call it the Golden. As in retriever."

It was a dog-hair fly, and I had to admit it had a nice foamy action in the water. Since Ray's academic specialty is canines, I shouldn't have been surprised. "I'm particularly interested in dogs and cultures," he once explained to me. "People in Zanzibar, for example, want absolutely nothing to do with dogs. Their local legend has it that dogs dug up and ate Muhammad right after he died. I guess if dogs ate your prophet, you wouldn't want much to do with them either. One of the strongest anti-dog taboos in the U.S. is among fly fishermen. They won't tie flies with dog fur, and I can't figure out why—it's cheap, accessible, and keeps your dog under control. Wave a pair of scissors and he's off the couch and down in the cellar. The fur has great movement in the water, too."

I don't know whether or not Ray's kidding half the time. But his tan dog-hair flies outfished my bright and flashy marabous that July morning. Apparently, he found the experience totally buoyant, for he took to tying dog-hair flies of all sorts and sizes, and dog-hair jigs, too. From all different species. He has subsequently used them to good advantage a number of times.

I haven't graduated to dog hair, but do use fuzzy or soft materials. Below is a dressing for a generic shallow-water streamer.

As for top-water choices, the Dahlberg Diver is a good pattern, and the above tie can be easily adapted to that pattern by substituting a clipped deer hair head for the Lite Brite. Be sure to keep a high deer hair collar in back of the head so that it pushes up water when retrieved. You can also use this same tie with a cork head—as either a slider or a popper. With all the patterns, I usually clip the bottom of the marabou to aid floating and/or hooking.

Best color depends on the forage base and water clarity. In the clear-water bays of the Great Lakes system, try white marabou with yellow or white saddle hackles (get the long, thin ones), and pearl Flashabou. If that doesn't work, try some chartreuse

---

### PATTERN 1: MARABOU PIKE STREAMER

**Hook** - Size 2, 8X long.
**Thread** - Monocord.
**Head** - White Lite Brite, dubbed.
**Eyes** - Red and black dumbbells or red and black stick-on.
**Hackle** - White and fluorescent yellow marabou, mixed with Holographic Flashabou.
**Tail** - Six white hackles, with pearl Flashabou.

*Instructions:*

1. For the tail, tie in the hackle feathers, flared.
2. Wind the marabou hackles, securing Holographic Flashabou so that it marries with the wound marabou hackle. Begin with a white feather, followed by a fluorescent yellow, followed by one or two white marabous. It may help to pinch flat the stem of the marabou hackles before securing them to the hook. Mix in three or four strands of Flashabou before each hackle so that the flash is evenly distributed.
3. Tie dumbbell eyes to the bottom of the hook (so that the fly rides in standard fashion). Use CA glue to secure the eyes to the hook, and finish with a Lite Brite head. If you're using stick-on eyes, apply after dubbing. Use Goop for extra adherence with stick-ons. I use fire red monocord to leave a splash of scarlet.

or blue in either the marabou or saddle hackle, and add some corresponding flash as well. Stained and marshy waters call for yellow, chartreuse, orange, black, and olive with gold or bronze Flashabou. In other words, fly color more or less parallels lure or plug color, water stain, and—to a lesser extent—forage base. A little splash of red never hurts.

Fly fishers do have one advantage in the action department, and that's in the materials themselves. Make your first, second, and third choices marabou. Pike absolutely love it. I've watched little ones in shallow water mesmerized by the breathing plumes. I tie almost all my pike flies with wound marabou hackles, Gartside-style. Most articles on pike flies stress durability—which should be stressed if you're spending a week at Wollaston Lake in Saskatchewan. But if you're hooking six or seven pike a day (which is a good day of fly fishing in the States), you're not concerned about them tearing up your gear. The limiting factor for me is seldom that pike ripped up my flies and I didn't have any left—in fact, happy day when that is the issue. No, my problem is usually the 30-incher that follows my streamer to the boat without striking, glares at me, and sinks back into the weeds.

Now, I'd very much like to catch that fish. I fully realize that its teeth might cost me a fly and probably the half hour of my time that it took to tie it. But I don't care. To paraphrase Robert Travers, given the amount of time I devote to unimportant things in my life, I consider that half hour nothing else but time well spent.

*A white marabou streamer is always a good starting choice for fly fishing. Note stripping basket.*

# PART III

## Summer

# 10

# Places of Plenty,
# Places of Few

As the July sun bakes the shorelines and bays, and surface temperatures rise through the 70s, adult pike move to deeper water where they can find comfortable levels of dissolved oxygen. Pike forage inconsistently during the warmer months, perhaps because ambushing opportunities are fewer in deep water. Fishing success falls off from the spring and early-summer period, too, although fishing pressure (particularly if you consider the incidental catches by anglers intent on other species) probably increases, which results in the demise of many small pike.

Serious pike fishermen look north. Pike have always symbolized the wilderness excursion; they are, after all, great *northern* pike. Nord. That's where the big ones swim.

## WHERE THE PIKE ARE

Whether in the northern United States, southern Canada, or at the northernmost edge of the pike's range, habitat matters. Pike become the major top-line predator in some waters; in others they share that role with bass, walleyes, or trout. Certain habitats offer advantages to northerns, and populations flourish; some habitats support only marginal populations.

- **Oligotrophic lakes,** noted mostly as salmonid habitat, also can sustain populations of pike. The overall habitat is infertile, but the water remains cold, with high levels of dissolved oxygen, so these waters tend to produce skeletal populations with bigger individual specimens. The pike have little competition, face less angling pressure in deep water, and can thus live long enough to attain trophy size. Most of the pike are caught in late winter (through the ice) or early spring.

- **Mesotrophic lakes** usually have an offshore cold-water fishery and an inshore warm-water fishery. These lakes (the Great Lakes fit into this category) are the top pike producers on the continent, with more weeds than the oligotrophic lakes and more cold-water depths than the eutrophic waters.

- **Eutrophic lakes** look like great habitat, which they are for some species. But not for pike. Any fishing pressure reduces the number of bigger fish, which inhibits cannibalism and leads to a lake full of 20-inch hammer handles. Low levels of dissolved oxygen prevent pike from expending the energy necessary to feed aggressively once the waters warm up in summer. Moreover, bluegills are often the chief forage, and they are tough for pike to catch even under the best conditions. Paradoxically, increasing angler harvest only leads to more and smaller pike.

- **Reservoirs** can have good pike fishing, particularly during filling, when water reaches vegetation of the previous year and results in good recruitment of young. Reservoirs may continue to produce, too, as is the case with prairie and western reservoirs that have enjoyed recent wet years. In addition to water depth, the keys to strong pike populations are diversity and size of weed habitats combined with dispersed fishing pressure or restricted limits. Canadian impoundments may have sparse weeds and good populations of pike, provided the fishing pressure is negligible.

- **Rivers** also support pike populations, so long as they meet the following criteria: weedy shallow backwaters for spawning and recruitment; shoreline weeds for nurseries for juvenile fish; and deep pools and oxygenated flows for summer survival of adult fish. Slow-moving rivers tend to have the most pike. The size of the pike will generally be a function of the size of the river and, in particular, the amount of fishing pressure.

- **Flows and ponds** also hold pike. Again, the characteristics necessary for a population include shallow weeds, feeding cover, and sufficient depth.

If certain habitats favor pike, the location of those habitats matters even more. In general, farther north means less fishing pressure and lower water temperatures—the two most important ingredients in maintaining a pike population.

*When the heat of summer drives civilized pike to deep water, many anglers turn their attention north. Ray Coppinger.*

Pike swim in many western states, and the reservoirs in Colorado, Montana, Iowa, Nebraska, and North and South Dakota offer some excellent fishing. Pike also inhabit heartland waters in Illinois, Indiana, Ohio, and, to the east, Pennsylvania and southern New England, but the fishing remains marginal, particularly in summer. You're better off heading north to the Great Lakes system. Minnesota, Wisconsin, and Michigan all have countless pike waters. Ditto for northern New York and Vermont. The fishing in these "border" states holds up into July, anyway.

Canada has the best angling. Reservoirs, rivers, and lakes across Quebec, Ontario, Manitoba, and Saskatchewan boast world-class pike fisheries, with some lightly fished, fly-in waters offering the possibility of many fish between 10 and 20 pounds. (Alaska waters probably belong in this group, too, national boundaries notwithstanding.) Drive-to waters get more pressure, naturally, though with enough vacation time, you can find some good ones.

The idea of heading into the wilds of Canada took root in the postwar years, once people had cleaned out the pike from the civilized part of the continent and the culture became suburbanized. Wealthy Americans took such trips to the Upper Peninsula, Adirondacks, and Maine in the previous century, and we still do today. But now, with improved modes of transportation, you can really indulge in a wilderness adventure.

## CANADIAN EXCURSIONS

The average size of pike increases as you work north, but you can still drive to good pike fishing. A few summers ago Ray Coppinger, Stan Warner, and I fished a reservoir some six hours north of Montreal, and it was loaded with pike in the 4- to 8-pound class, with a 12- and a 15-pounder rounding off the bigger fish. Other lakes across Quebec and Ontario offer such possibilities, too. Before setting out, contact the province you intend to fish. Get a read on the best areas to try. Check regulations, too, as guides are necessary once you reach a certain point north.

If you want to do it yourself, pay particular attention to Ray and Stan's motto: *No Walleyes.* That is, lakes without walleyes receive the least fishing pressure. Naturally, you need to bring backups to everything—boating essentials, spare tires for truck and trailer, tools, extra 3- to 6-horse engine, and so on. Also, back up your fishing essentials with extra reels, line, packs of wire leaders (definitely, because they twist even if you don't lose them), pliers, jaw spreaders, knife, bug dope, head net, rain suit (including pants), and gloves for handling fish.

Stan and Ray have academic research projects that take them to the greatest pike fishing in eastern Canada. That great trophy-pike fisherman, the late Bill Tenny, chased big northerns around the world, not just around a province as Stan and Ray do. But the same spirit moves all three and other adventuresome souls who would bargain with the devil himself to land that 47-pounder. But for most of us, vacation time comes at a premium. The practical approach to fishing northern Canada is to book a week in a lodge. Naturally, this sort of trip requires considerable research. Contacts can be gleaned from magazine articles and advertisements, guidebooks, sports shows, and various provincial governments. Get the brochures, interview the owners. Talk to people who have fished there. Explain that you want to catch northerns (not walleyes). Pike. *Grand brochet,* not *doré.* Explain the kind of fishing you'd like to do—fly fishing, for instance. Make your plans in advance, during the fall or early winter. Plan to spend some money, too; this sort of vacation doesn't come cheap.

*Some anglers prefer to do it themselves, by wilderness camping. If so, bring extras of everything, gas included. Ray Coppinger.*

Civilized gear and strategies will catch wilderness fish, but the tackle often won't stand up under the wear and tear of 20 to 30 big pike per day. You always end up needing more terminal tackle (leaders, spoons, heavy-duty bucktail spinners, and streamers) than you have.

Forget about all the permutations of various lures; take some basic types with plenty of backups. If the lodge owner says that yellow and red spoons are good, take a box of them. You may not have an opportunity to restock. Take along a backup reel and rod. Most lodges will explain what's available and what isn't, but this information is worth checking.

If you're going to err, do so on the side of heavy rather than light. Storms in the Canadian north can have you looking for pairs of animals and an ark. You need a full rain suit. You also want bug dope, sunscreen, and at least two pairs of polarized glasses. If you fly fish, the opportunities for restocking are fewer than if you're using spin tackle. You definitely want to bring a backup fly rod and reel and pretie your leaders. I pack a basic fly-tying kit, as well.

Wherever fishing pressure is minimal or strict conservation measures are in place, wilderness fishing continues to be an out-of-this-world experience. By the same token, fishing pressure has had a profound impact on pike fisheries in the United States and southern and central Canada. In fact, one study analyzed the fossils from archaeological finds with the idea of getting a glimpse of what the fishing was like before fishing with a hook and line was invented. Both pike perch (walleyes) and northerns were bigger then, and it made me feel good because now I know all those old-timers aren't lying.

## PIKE CONSERVATION

A very big pike in Canada is 30 pounds, a big one 20 pounds, a decent fish 10; divide in half for the United States. Certain American waters do permit pike to reach 20 pounds or more, but these are oligotrophic lakes and reservoirs with limited (read: impossible to catch) populations. For the most part the best U.S. fisheries have good numbers of adult fish in the 5- to 12-pound range. If the pike in your favorite lake average this size, count yourself lucky, keep quiet, and hope your local fisheries manager resists the temptation to stock the water with walleyes.

The reason for the disparity between civilized pike and wilderness pike? Simple. Pike populations are highly vulnerable to angling pressure. A 1972 study found that two anglers caught 28 percent of the pike population in a lake in just 11 hours of fishing. It seems obvious, but I can't help thinking that the impact of fishing pressure gets overlooked. So I'll risk sounding moronic and put it plain: Pike that get fished and kept don't get big. Pike grow quickly in the U.S. waters, but they get caught. In contrast, it takes 10 years to grow a 20-inch pike in lakes to the Far North, but they can live that long in the absence of fishing pressure, which is what accounts for the big pike up there; it certainly isn't the fertility of the lakes.

Fishing pressure skims off the biggest pike, and virtually every study on the subject confirms the point. Data from an important study on Heming Lake in Manitoba show that the frequency of fish larger than 20 inches fell sharply during years of high fishing effort. Netting surveys also found decreases in average length and weight. When intensive fishing stopped in 1961, the size of fish in nets increased.

Every lake or water has differences, of course, and huge fisheries like the Great Lakes have dynamics nobody understands. But the general scenario for most pike populations goes as follows: Anglers remove bigger fish, so the smaller northerns experience less predation. Their increased numbers in turn lead to excessive predation on perch and baitfish populations, leading to a rise in bluegill populations, since perch aren't there to eat the sunfish. The northerns have a tough time catching bigger bluegills and rely on smaller ones. As more northerns are caught, their numbers only increase, and their growth rate diminishes. Hammer-handle time.

Even eutrophic waters can sustain reasonable pike populations, if the big pike are returned to the water. When they're not, the pike populations explode and sizes diminish. A good example occurred on Perch Lake near the Canadian border. The New York State Department of Environmental Conservation bought Perch Lake many years ago under the conditions that no fishing would be permitted, because the owner had exclusive fishing rights to the lake. His lease expired in 1994. Perch Lake by law could now be fished.

There was just one problem. The lake turned out to be a nesting site for bald eagles, so wildlife managers prohibited fishing, for fear of disturbing the birds. Never mind that the bald eagles some 10 miles away on Tibbets Point on Lake Ontario appeared oblivious to human presence.

*A slim pike from a eutrophic pond in northern New York.*

You would think a compromise could've been worked out on Perch Lake: canoes-only, fishing just three days a week, or what have you. It would have been the perfect opportunity to manage a catch-and-release fishery for pike and largemouths. But that wasn't considered. (You wonder if an accommodation could have been reached had the lake been filled with brook trout or walleyes.) And it's not like the fisheries biologists didn't try. The wildlife managers simply wouldn't hear of it.

The solution? Ice fish 'em. This "accommodation" fit in perfectly with the pike's niche. That is, the pike play a peripheral role in a fishery that revolves around bass, salmonids, walleyes, and muskies—except in the winter, when those species are largely unavailable. Ice fishing. Perfect! The anglers wouldn't disturb the eagles, and sportsmen could put the boots to all the pike they wanted.

The netting surveys the year before ice fishing was instituted showed pike topping off at 13 pounds, with the population in pretty typical age structure. The first year of ice fishing took care of most of the larger fish. The second year of ice fishing found smaller pike, as you'd expect, until they too were gone, leaving a lake full of hammer handles (with a few large pike). In other words, it wasn't the eutrophic nature of the water that skewed the population, it was the combination of eutrophic water and fishing pressure. It depresses me to think how often this scenario has been replayed across the pike's range.

All the more reason to do what we can to protect populations of northerns. But most state agencies have little interest in pike, as northerns don't generate the revenues that walleyes, bass, and salmonids do. I'm not referring to fisheries biologists, many of whom have sought for years to educate sportsman's groups about the value of pike, but to the larger powers that be in the state fish and wildlife agencies, whose sole interest in northerns is to squeeze whatever tourist dollars they can out of pike-hungry visitors. Why anybody needs to take home five pike is beyond me, but most traditional pike-fishing states have such liberal limits, ensuring that we will see money-back guarantees on fishing licenses before we see a return to reasonable numbers of big fish in our best natural pike lakes.

Pike enjoy more appreciation on the periphery of their range due to their exotic status. The deeper you get into the pike's indigenous range, the less benign the attitudes about them, a remnant of the old 19th-century get-rid-of-the-varmint mentality. We see this with pike shooting on Lake Champlain; we see it with pike spearing in Michigan, Wisconsin, and Minnesota; we see it with ice-fishing "derbies" in New York; and we see it in assumptions of the pike-management practices in these traditional pike states. States with trout-fishing traditions often respond in kind, even if not part of the indigenous range; Montana, for instance, allows anglers to keep 10 pike per day. These are the areas in which pike could thrive, which I suppose is why the local angling communities assume such a retro stance toward them. Some pike are fine. But a lot of big ones? Well.

The attitude about pike, as we have seen, is inextricably a part of our culture, deeper than simply a matter of pike eating all the brook trout. It's how they do it, what they look like doing it. Their choppers, for one thing. In general, the bigger the teeth, the less favorable the human response—particularly in fish. Start with sharks and work through piranhas, barracudas, and pickerel to favored fish such as bass and trout. (The exception to the toothiness rule is the muskellunge, which is the king—at least in size—of fresh water.) You never hear of bass or trout being called "mean" or "vicious" or "terrors."

These beliefs result in the "rid them" attitude that fueled early efforts to eliminate pike, like any other varmint, and that still linger in everyday perceptions. Think about it: The trout angler in our culture reports an empathy for and veneration of the individual fish. The angler becomes a part of nature—if he is a good fisherman—and the relationship between fish and the human becomes a cause for celebration. But pike preclude such a relationship—they're too vicious. Wolves don't make good pets.

All of which makes for exciting fishing, but a much tougher row to hoe when we consider the question of pike conservation. That's the problem—attitude, not feasibility. We've known for centuries, literally, that conservation works. When the harvest of pike, for both food and sport, increased in the 11th and 12th centuries, King Philip IV of France had the good sense to impose regulations governing seasons and tackle: No pike worth less than two denier could be taken. It would be nice to say that after 1,000 years, pike conservation is an idea whose time has come, but I wouldn't put too much denier on it.

This attitude has been around for years, although it is less acted upon than it used to be. What makes this more benign version so insidious is that it gets camouflaged by the fact that the numbers of pike *fans* are increasing. Maybe it has to do with the age of identity politics. Maybe it has do with our reverence for anything wild and unpredictable in this age of artificial fisheries. Whatever the reason, interest has grown, which has meant two things: an analgesic effect that comes from more people saying pike are good, and more fishing pressure from better fishermen. Meanwhile, the attitudes that inform the legislation governing pike fishing, the attitudes that influence how anglers actually treat pike when they comply with the very minimal rules, remain the same. That's the problem with pike shooting and pike spearing: It's tough to get anglers to release pike gently if you can spear them in the next lake over, or a month later shoot the same pike with a deer rifle.

When done properly, catch-and-release works—that's the shame. In one study lightly hooked pike totaled 98 percent of those caught on spinners and 83 percent of those caught on live bait. Both categories, whether single-hooked on live bait or tre-ble-hooked on spinners, showed low mortality in a follow-up study six months later (2 percent on treble hooks/spinners, 6 percent on single hooks/live bait). A different experiment looked at pike that swallowed the hook. Researchers cut the line and re-leased the fish. Six months later these fish also showed relatively low mortality (13 percent). Deeply hooked pike were dissected, and some 60 percent of the swallowed hooks had disappeared—54 percent of the trebles, 62 percent of the singles. Pike that had swallowed hooks had a growth rate equal to other pike in the test water.

A Manitoba and Missouri study conducted in 1977 showed mortality on artifi-cials with barbed trebles varying from 1.7 to 5.3 percent, and mortality on barbless (lure hooks) to be 10.5 percent, perhaps because the barbless hook found a deeper set. For the record, I am a barbless fan and pinch down all the barbs on my pike lures: A released pike stands the best chance for survival when it is returned to the water as quickly and gently as possible, and a barbless hook (or hooks) definitely ex-acerbates the process. A barbless hook also means that I don't end up doing a Siamese twin routine with a pike on some Canadian lake while Lassie is off looking for the local wilderness doctor.

Whatever the particulars, catch-and-release remains a highly effective, if sadly underutilized, management tool. Popular Canadian pike waters—Wollaston Lake in Saskatchewan is a good example—often have strict regulations that require catch-and-release and single barbless hooks. Camp owners in the wilderness, of course, have a real interest in keeping the pike big in their lakes; elsewhere, that interest sim-ply doesn't exist, except with those of us who wouldn't mind some quality northern fishing. All the more reason for pike anglers to take the lead with catch-and-release, with keeping the pressure on state agencies to manage pike like they manage other fish. All the more reason to join Pikemasters, which continues to print the truth about pike conservation (or the lack thereof), and which continues to lobby for restrictions on limits and lengths, for appreciation of pike as gamefish, for a commitment to im-proving pike habitat.

Pikemasters
P.O. Box 414
Marshall, MI 49068
http://www.tttoutdoors.com
http://www.sportsmanweb.com

Increasing numbers of anglers do take care with releasing their catch these days, and incidentally caught pike today receive better treatment than those caught a gener-ation ago, when they were unceremoniously thrown on the bank with suckers, bass, and anything else without luminous eyes or bright spots. Nevertheless, pike still don't get the gentle treatment that helps with survival. Pike have big teeth and thrash in the boat, leaving the impression that they are impervious to injury. Funny how when you have them on a stringer with smallmouths or walleyes, northerns are always the first to die.

The least-intrusive way to land a northern? Maneuver it to a position beside the boat, keeping pressure on the line, and grasp the pike across the back just at the rear of the gills. Then, laying down your rod, pick up the needle-nose pliers and use them to twist out the lure. Pike often take lures deeply, making noninvasive procedures impossible. Ditto for pike that get to 10 or 12 pounds. In either case, use a boat net or a cradle to immobilize the pike in the mesh against the side (outside if possible, but inside if necessary) of the boat while the lure is extracted. This maneuver sometimes

*Pike up to this size (12–14 pounds) can be landed, behind the head and across the gill plates. The key with hand landing pike is to tire the fish, keep the line taut, and grasp firmly.*

requires help, and if this can be done with a minimum of slime removal, so much the better. Jaw spreaders help a good deal—are imperative if you're fishing alone—and needle-nose pliers are essential.

No doubt about it, northerns are tough to handle. Nobody wants to get too close to their teeth, and a pike in a boat is as slippery as an eel at midnight. The bowling-ball grip, so called because the angler grabbed the northern by the eye sockets with thumb and forefinger, comprised the proper way to handle a northern for years. These days anglers grip small to moderate-sized fish (under 12 pounds) across the back at the rear of the gill plates, although it is important to avoid the gills, which can seriously injure both parties. Pike can also be held by slipping a finger under the chin just beneath the jaw, though again care should be taken that fingers don't slip into the gills.

In any case, the important point is to return the pike to the water quickly. Give it a little squeeze just behind the rear fins and often as not it will zoom out of sight.

## CIVILIZED PIKE

We delight in stories that highlight the pike's bold behavior. One of my favorites comes from Ray Coppinger, who tells of the 5-pound pike that grabbed the Little Cleo spoon dangling from his rod on his backcast. Ray was fishing in northern Quebec. This pike had never seen an artificial lure in its slimy little life.

Back in the early 1980s my old friend Pete Bellinger and I were pike fishing in the St. Lawrence River. I had just caught a small bluegill on a plastic grub and a 15- to 16-inch pike materialized from the green depths, nipping at the tail of the sunfish as I reeled it to the boat. The pike grabbed it within our sight and remained right there, but refused to cede me the fish even as I slowly pulled in the both of them. Pete eased the net beneath the pair and lifted. The pike let go at that point (finally!), and moments later we released the sunfish and the pike—each on its own side of the boat.

To me, these instances reflect the behavioral differences between Canadian and American pike. The "country" (Canadian) pike remain innocent longer; the "city" (American) pike grow up quicker. At 15 or 16 inches the St. Lawrence River pike was probably three years old. Perhaps that fish had never had an angling experience, either. But I think it is fair to say that a 5-pound pike in the St. Lawrence would never have acted that way.

These differences have, in effect, created two different fish, at least as far as appropriate angling strategies are concerned. As noted, civilized gear won't stand up under the stresses and strains of wilderness excursions. For different reasons, wilderness strategies and gear prove just as inadequate for "civilized" pike. These fish see a

*A wide landing net can be used, as well, though care should be taken to minimize thrashing which removes slime.*

parade of lures every day. After the population gets fished down, fewer good-sized pike will remain. Suffice it to say that they are on their guard. These are not the fierce, eat-anything-that-moves 30-pound pike of Canadian legend; these are skittish 30-inchers that slip back into weeds when a shadow crosses their vision.

For years, however, wilderness tactics have dominated pike fishing, in part because the wilderness strategy remains close to the traditional pike strategy, formed when there was little fishing pressure on American and southern Canadian waters, and in part because of the economics of the sport-fishing industry. That is, outdoor writer goes on a free trip to a Canadian lake where pike grow old without ever seeing a lure and the water temperature remains cool enough to keep the pike in the shallows all summer. He cleans up on Five of Diamonds Dardevles—on any spoon, for that matter, the brighter, the better. The flashy lures catch one pike after another.

The writer owes the lodge an article. And he writes one about the "Water Wolves of the North Country." This slant fits neatly with the way pike have been constructed within the angling community; not many magazines are interested in stories about the 5- to 6-pound pike that come out of public waters in the States. The writer tells the truth, too—the pike hit spoons as quick as they hit the water—color, size, didn't matter. The fish were simply ferocious. And so the deal is done: Wilderness strategy becomes *the* strategy. The result is the familiar how-to-catch-pike drivel that doesn't work unless you're going to northern Canada or time traveling back to the 19th century.

Without a doubt, pike throughout the range share a good deal in terms of behavior, habitat, and response to conditions. Nevertheless, the results from the traditional methods leave much to be desired in waters closer to civilization—even if we understand how they have evolved, how they reflect our larger cultural assumptions about fierce pike being unafraid of humans. Like successful angling of any kind, details matter, and these details become absolutely crucial during the summer months, when the points of comparison involve never-fished pike in cool waters of northern Canada and heavily fished pike in warm waters of the United States and southern Canada. If summer fishing in clear water means tough fishing for walleyes, trout, bass, muskies, and any other gamefish, can you think of a reason why pike should be excepted from that list?

Indeed, I would make the case that pike are the toughest of them all.

# 11

# Heat

The warm-water aquaria of summer shallows. Clouds of tadpoles shivering through the grasses. Bluegills arranging themselves beneath weed mats like models on a mobile. Largemouth bass, few in number but substantial in presence, waiting for the patter above that betrays a hopping frog on the pads.

Pods of shiners turn in the sun, and the panfish and small bass plow into them. Families of mallards paddle about like out-of-work actors, looking to entertain in exchange for food. Swimmers and skiers shriek and splash through the shallows, outdone only by the head-splitting whine of the North American jet ski. It is mid-July, and pike lakes hum with the fertility of the North Country's kindest season.

The pike are nowhere to be found.

In their traditionally casual approach to fishing for northerns, anglers never realized that little truth. Pike lived in the weeds and devoured anything foolish enough to venture within range. Period. Their all-consuming ferocity canceled out any good sense, so they never knew enough to vacate the hot-tub shallows like trout, bass, walleyes—even catfish, for that matter. After all, this weedbed held a pike every 10 yards back in May and June. It wasn't like they pulled up and left.

And so the company line: There were times when pike just couldn't be caught, and summer was one of them. There wasn't much you could do about it, either, a fact I resigned myself to on a crisp, late-summer evening many years ago. I was a boy, camping in a state park on the St. Lawrence River, listening quietly as the resident pike expert held forth in the orange light of a campfire.

"You're just going to have to wait until fall to catch pike," he said. "They couldn't bite now if they wanted to."

Someone asked him why.

"No teeth." He let the pronouncement hang there in the cedar smoke. "Their gums soften up when it gets hot, and they drop their teeth. Then they grow 'em back in fall when the water cools down."

Small wonder I couldn't catch any pike. The no-teeth thing explained my poor luck fishing suckers on bobbers and casting Dardevles. But what about the occasional pike that came my way while drifting shiners for smallmouths off a certain deep weedline? Oddballs probably. On-purpose pike fishing meant finding a weedbed, throwing out a sucker and a bobber or maybe flinging around a big Dardevle. Once the pike got their teeth back, they'd grab either one in a hurry.

It would be at least 10 years before I would enjoy any success with summer northerns, and it wasn't for a lack of trying.

## SUMMER SUCKER

Lakeview Marsh, just a barrier beach from the broadest reaches of Lake Ontario, had a reputation for big pike, and in retrospect I can see why. The tire-sized snapping turtles, arm-thick water snakes, and impenetrable weeds really appealed to the pike in our imagination. If a fish liked weeds—and that was one thing pike liked—this was the place to live. Anglers would come back from plugging for bass with wild tales of big pike. My dad, who worked nearby during the summer, got me the inside info: bass back in the weeds, northerns in the channel where the creek hit the marsh.

One evening a friend and I found the juncture of the creek and marsh and then backed up the creek to the biggest hole with the most cover. I set out three poles for us, each with a sucker and bobber, then sat back to enjoy the evening. Another Lake Ontario pastel, with etchings of fair-weather clouds stretching across a sherbet skyline. Just before dark, one of the bobbers twitched. A few years later I would be reminded of this moment when I saw the movie *Jaws,* specifically the scene on the boat in which the reel clicks twice and Quint looks down at it, understanding what is happening, while Roy Scheider blithers on about a bowline. My friend, B. J., was no more a pike angler than Scheider was a sailor, and he was likewise oblivious to the impending drama. I watched the bobber twitch again, skate across the surface, and then disappear. I flipped the bail on the reel and the mono looped off.

"Hey, is that a bite?"

*A narrow, weedy point extending into deep water is an excellent summer location. This angler works down the main body side of the point before trying the deep end of the shoal (the underwater extension of the point) and then moving into the bay side. A depthfinder is invaluable for this sort of work.*

"That would be my guess," I said, watching as the line moved toward the shore. Ten minutes later I laid into that fish, and it was like hooking a retaining wall. Whatever was on the other end headed for a downed willow tree some 30 feet away. I screwed down the drag in hopes of turning the fish, felt the line stretch, and *snnaapp!*

A week later we were back, spooled up with some serious cable. We anchored farther up in the creek, a washed-out pool close to 15 feet deep. B. J. had a bite and missed it. A third companion was with us, as well, a talker who'd "done a lot of pike fishing."

The pike were there, and I caught two of them. They were not only the biggest pike I'd ever caught but the biggest ones I'd ever seen. Both took suckers, swallowing the hook out of sight. After fishing we stopped at my dad's, and he weighed the pike.

In the yellowy garage light the scale read 17 pounds for one and 13 and change for the other. This called for some serious bragging, B. J. and I agreed, and our third friend came along, quiet, on the polite side of sulking. We headed out to a lakeside bar where we ran into our friend Bob Charlebois. B. J. told him about the pike.

"That must have been great," Bob said to me. "Those are good-sized north—"

"Well, it's not like they can fight a lot," our third fellow from the boat cut in. "I mean they swallowed the hook. They were hooked deep in the gut."

At the time I passed off the comment to that's just the way he was, competitive, intense. In retrospect he was quite right.

The "great fisherman" is a pose, of course, but at 21 I was too full of myself to perceive its hollow construction. I spent the following August in Shelburne Bay on Lake Champlain, poling and rowing my skiff along weed edges. I had the perfect suckers—8-inchers, fat and shiny. Tethered them on two poles out the back. I was an expert at catching big pike.

I may have landed three pike in 30 hours of fishing, the biggest reaching a full 22 inches. When I finally did manage a pike of 10 pounds that August, it came out of deep water where I was smallmouth fishing. I'd come full circle, back to my days on the St. Lawrence River and lessons at the campfire.

## LOCATION

The following June I'd have a pike belly conversion experience some 10 miles to the south on Little Otter Creek that would once and for all open my eyes to the actual fun of fishing for pike, as opposed to the desperate glory of driving around from bar to bar with big dead ones in the trunk. And that was no small epiphany, for those of you scoring at home. But it would be awhile before I came to understand pike during the summer, before I realized that pike don't drop their teeth, but instead go—teeth and all—to where the water is cool and dissolved oxygen at a sufficient level. Green weed growth helps with oxygen levels, too. But if the pike are ever to get much beyond 10 pounds, they need temperatures between 55 and 65 degrees.

There's no rule to finding those temperatures. But here's a start, what I call the rule of doubles and halves—5 feet in May, 10 feet in June, 20 feet in July and August, 10 feet in September, and 5 feet in October. These are starting points, with all other things (weeds, forage, clarity) being equal, and assume a midrange location (southern Canada, Vermont, New York, Michigan, Wisconsin, Minnesota, Montana, Nebraska, Iowa, Dakotas, Colorado) for pike in the 5- to 12-pound class. Summer pike might drop down to the 20- or even 30-foot depths during the day, but move to the top of a weedy shoal during low light or as a front approaches. There may be other movement in big waters early in the morning and late in the afternoon.

Summer is a good time to fish rivers, given sufficient levels. The water runs reasonably clear, the fish likely to be in predictable places—big pools below water falls, deep slack water next to heavily oxygenated sections, shaded pools—particularly if that pool is the deepest in a given stretch of water (which was why those big northerns were in that particular channel back in Lakeview Marsh). Chuck Ringer, son of my pike belly buddy, Ralph, used to get some nice northerns every July in Big Otter Creek right in the middle of the Vermont town of Vergennes, by "walk trolling" Rapalas beneath an undercut bank. His favorite spot combined all three of the above criteria: base of falls, deepest pool, and shaded area. No wonder that spot was loaded with pike.

In lakes, transitions in weed density may be very important in early June, but transitions in depth become increasingly important by the end of the month. Proximity to deep water, relatively important for big fish throughout the season, is absolutely vital during the warm months. Such a location gives pike options. Signifcant, as rescarch indicates that bigger pike can use more habitat than smaller pike. If you find a dense weedline on a shelf that drops from 8 to 15 feet, then tapers into a wider area of weeds in 25 feet of water that eventually falls to 40 feet or more, you have an excellent area to fish for summer pike.

Shallow weeds may still hold pike in the 18- to 26-inch range. Pike between 5 and 10 pounds seem drawn to deeper water, though not to the extent of larger pike, which can't feed without it and simply have no energy to chase in warm water. They

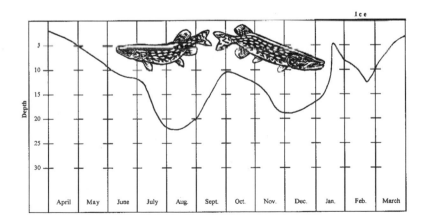

*Pike movement through the year.*

remain unable to hunt the shallows where the panfish concentrate, because the water temperature can be 80 degrees or more. So they take what they can get from a deep-water hideout, aware on some level that they only get one shot at their target. They watch and wait for something they "know" they can catch: the alewife or smelt that can't keep up with the school; the disoriented perch; the small walleye or smallmouth that swims erratically.

If anything, pike may go deeper than ever these days, particularly in the Great Lakes and associated waters that have clarified markedly due to the elimination of phosphates and influx of zebra mussels. My little boy, Brody, caught his first pike in August 1995, and it came from 43 feet of water. My first pike, in August 1958, came from 4.

## SUMMER PRESENTATIONS

A number of the standard presentations are worth trying in the summer. When pike move up on an weedy offshore shoal before a front, you can get them on a spinnerbait and trailer. The spinnerbait makes a good searching lure, because you can experiment with presentations. As noted in chapter 7, pike often have stronger preferences regarding lure "behavior" than color, shape, or size. Retrieve it steadily, pump it, or

*Deep running plugs like this Wally Diver make excellent summer lures.*

start and stop it. Some anglers prefer the in-line spinners with bucktails, particularly later in the summer. With bigger, heavier models you can reach the deeper pockets of 15 to 20 feet.

Other deep, horizontal strategies work, too, such as casting crankbaits or deep-running plugs. Drifting a live shiner on a light line is another reliable approach. St. Lawrence River guide Al Benas has made a career out of using 5-foot rods and 6-pound test to drift shiners through the 15- to 25-foot depths. And he always catches pike. He'd better.

Drifting shows the bait to a lot of fish, but summer pike often want a bit of speed to the deep horizontal presentations. Deep trolling accomplishes both. If you troll spoons at a good clip, they spin rather than wobble, and they rise off the bottom, as well. Weighted spinners or spinnerbaits can be trolled at a good clip, but my preference is for the lipped crankbaits. They offer a realistic forage imitation. Best of all, the faster you troll, the deeper they dive, offering that mix of realistic forage, speed, and depth that can be critical during summer–late summer.

The Shad Raps and Wally Divers will dig down to the 15-foot-plus range. You can get down to 20 and 25 feet with the Mann's Stretch plugs. My favorite trolling lure is the C.C. Rattlin' Shad. It doesn't run quite as deep as some plugs, but with 6-pound test and a long trolling line, you can squeeze out a little extra depth. Remember that the diameter of the line has an important effect on crankbait depth: 4-pound-test line lets the crankbait run deeper than 6-pound test, which gets it deeper than 8-pound test, and so on. Light line, in other words, keeps that crankbait swimming by every pike on the weedline.

My friend Lee Ellsworth and I troll deep weedlines in Henderson Bay on Lake Ontario quite a bit during the late summer, and we do pretty well at it. These weeds fall off from 8 feet to about 20, and the vegetation covers the entire drop-off, as it does the 20-foot bottom. The pike plaster themselves to the drop-off, and we try to drag our plugs right past their noses. We've come to know the points and dips pretty well over the years and can cut things pretty fine.

There's more to trolling than the right location, however. I'll never forget one quiet summer evening when a boat appeared off to the side, headed right for us. Lee shifted into neutral so we could let it pass.

"Tourists," Lee said, as we drifted to a stop, "not a rod in sight. I don't think they know we're trolling. Or fishing, for that matter."

They waved, one of them took a picture, and we waved back again. Lee put the boat in gear. Immediately my rod plunged to the water, and I felt the hard lunges of a nice pike. It rolled to the surface, drawing *oohs!* and *ahs!* from the other boat. Now they really started taking pictures. After I landed the pike, they even asked me to pose with it, which I did complaining about the slime to Lee while manufacturing a smile

*Deep trolling will take pike during hot weather in the middle of the day. This pike came from an off-shore weed bed in the Great Lakes.*

for the camera. "Serves you right," he laughed. "You've been torturing your friends for years, making us hold all kinds of fish for photos that we never get to see. How do you like it?"

Our friends in the other boat moved on to gentler vistas, and I slipped the fat pike over the side. Seven, maybe 8 pounds, it had been chowing down along that deep weed-line all summer. My crankbait must have come wobbling by the weedbed at a slow, catchable speed. Perhaps another pike started after it, but let it pass. Farther down the weedline the plug may have come really close to my pike, which just couldn't resist following. Suddenly the minnow stopped swimming and the pike virtually ran over it. Then that minnow just took off diving for the bottom. Well, we can't have that. Snap!

I pointed this out to Lee. He shrugged. "Who knows?" he said. "You've certainly had weirder theories."

He started the engine. We settled into trolling again, lulled by the steady thrum of the crankbaits. Suddenly the boat fell into neutral—just as we were reaching a yellow

*This angler is trolling deep-running minnow plugs, taking care to remain right on the edge of a weedy drop-off. Although close to shore, this weed edge runs from 18–30 feet.*

cottage, which was our shoreline mark for a small hump that often held fish. I looked back at Lee. He was sitting there waiting, his line growing slack. Mine was, too, as the crankbaits rose toward the surface.

"Just testing out the theory," he said. "Ready?" He shifted into gear. We went maybe 10 feet, and Lee's rod bowed, revealing the slow thump of a good northern. Yes!

Typical late-summer pike. They'd seen a lot of fishermen, a lot of lures, a lot of everything. They'd been exposed to it all; overexposed, actually. You really could call them wary fish. Catching them required a deep-water presentation with a realistic bait that imitated a vulnerable forage. And, as Lee noted later, a little extra help from the local tourist trade didn't hurt one bit.

## VERTICAL PRESENTATION

Spoons are never a bad choice for northerns. In the waters of the Far North you can cast Five of Diamonds and red and white Dardevles from ice-out to ice-in and catch fish every day. Working them with a "flutter retrieve," as described in chapter 5, can be a deadly summertime strategy on lakes in southern Canada and the northern United States, too. So manipulated, these spoons offer the perfect imitation of a vulnerable, pelagic baitfish.

For the most part, Little Cleos get the nod for this sort of work, particularly in clear water. In stained water a Red Eye Wiggler in chartreuse, fluorescent orange, or Fire Tiger gets the starting assignment. In either case, it pays to experiment with spoon sizes. My general inclination is start big then try increasingly smaller spoons until one provokes a strike.

You can use heavy jigging spoons, but I have never found these effective on pike. They don't seem to have the fluttering action so important to this presentation. If I have a hard time getting down, I'll either toss the spoon more directly updrift or change spools to lighter lines. With deep-water pike, you seldom have to worry about obstructions. I often use 6-pound test.

If anything the slower drop makes the strategy more effective. A wide spoon (Dardevle, Thomas Buoyant, Red Eye Wiggler, Little Cleo, etc.) gives the most action and can be terrific on a slow, lazy retrieve, with plenty of pauses. Lightweight spoons offer the slowest retrieve of all, and I've used 5-inch-long Suttons on 4-pound to take stubborn late-summer pike. Sometimes it would take five minutes to fish out a cast, as even a slight pull would result in a marked hop up in the water column. Detecting strikes was difficult. Often they'd come as a little added pressure to the drop. The trick was to keep the line just on the slack side of taut—and be ready to strike.

Lead-headed jigs work well, too, and I've probably caught more summer pike on them than any other lure or bait. Jigs have also taught me a great deal about the role of lure behavior and action in hooking a pike, which in turn led me to a fuller appreciation of the pike as a gamefish.

Back in the early 1980s, I began to try to write articles for fishing magazines. As far as I could tell, breaking into this field required that I come up with something new, offbeat. *Outdoor Life* was not going to assign me a piece on surface fishing for largemouths, for instance, when a dozen different TV personalities could do the same piece, and do it better. Pike were a different story—nobody famous fished for them, but guys in Massachusetts, Connecticut, and New Jersey (places where there weren't any pike, in other words) would give anything to catch one. So I adjusted my sights accordingly. Pike it was.

Spending summers on the St. Lawrence River, I started fooling around with jigs and northerns. My fishing buddies all liked to catch smallmouth bass, so most of the time I was fishing over drop-offs in the St. Lawrence with Mister Twisters, the hot lure of the early 1980s. I ended up catching quite a few smallmouths, and quite a few pike, too. Upon adding a rubber worm to the jighead, I caught even more of them.

So I proposed an article on using plastic worms to catch northerns to *Field & Stream*. The editor liked it, but it turns out he was running a "twister" article on walleyes, a "grub" article on smallmouths, and a "worm" article on largemouths. "One more rubber piece, you'll be able to dribble this damn issue home," he said. "Got any other ideas?"

I knew two other ways to catch pike besides plastic worms: sucker minnows and bobbers, and pike bellies. The pike bellies had a nice slant, since I'd first read about them 25 years earlier in the same magazine, thanks to H. G. Tapply's "Sportsman's Notebook." I sent in an article proposal and the editor passed it along to the guy in charge of the fishing annual, who gave me a go-ahead as long as "the tactics described work throughout the season and good pictures accompany the article."

I wondered what to call my TV show. Then I realized this could be tricky. The piece was due at the end of August, and I had no pictures. How on earth do you catch pike in mid-August on pike bellies? Maybe I could hook them to a jighead? Northerns certainly liked plastic worms rigged that way; they took jigs with minnow, too. I phoned Al Benas, who had a 30-foot driftboat that accommodated some 10 to 12 customers off the back. I told him what I needed. Silence on the other end. Then he agreed to let me come out, "so long as you fish off the bow and don't scare off the paying customers. And you gotta ask 'em before you start slicing up their fish."

On the day's first drift one of Al's sports caught a pike on a shiner. Al asked him if I could take just a little slice off the belly. The guy looked at Al, then me. But he nodded. "Okay."

I went into the cabin, did some surgery, and emerged with the belly meat hooked to a jig. We were fishing in 30 feet of water, and the drift had increased thanks to a building southwest wind.

"Let out a little more line," Al called to the anglers. I did as well and felt resistance on the line, heavy resistance that pulled mono from the drag. Oops, too much line. Then there were those slow, delicious tugs. Nope, just right.

As it turned out, the visitor was a 6-pound pike. A couple of other folks tried the pike bellies and jigs, and they caught pike on them, too. I got my pictures, which appeared in the 1986 *Field & Stream Fishing Annual* with my article. I have Al Benas, jigs, and pike bellies to thank for that bit of good fortune. And not to break my string, I sold the plastic-worm, deep-water-pike piece to the 1987 *Outdoor Life Fishing Annual*. After that I ran out of things to put on jigs, say nothing of fishing annuals that would buy my stories.

*A jig and pike belly accounted for this toothy critter.*

But jigs work. If I could use only one pike lure during July and August, it would be a jig and trailer. The only limitation is shallow water. When fishing in depths under 10 feet, I turn to a heavy spinnerbait and trailer, for all intents and purposes a jig with a spinner on top. Consistent with their interest in struggling forage fish, pike prefer jigs with a swimming stop-and-drop motion over those with a twitching hop, hop, hop that appeals to crayfish-oriented bass. Unlike spoons, which probably imitate an injured or dying minnow, jigs dive to the bottom and imitate live, swimming minnows. This avoidance behavior is typical of pike prey, which is probably why so many strikes occur during or right after the jig drops.

As with hardware, jigs benefit from light line in the 6-pound class, because the thin diameter accentuates the falling motion. The exception is fishing the bends of rivers, where pike often hold next to a sunken tree. Here you want all the muscle you can muster, as my friend Bob McNitt will tell you after his experience with a big northern on our annual summer float trip several years ago. It was the fish of the trip and McNitt hooked the pike, as he recalled after returning to camp, "right next to a tree branch on 17-pound test. I had him on for all of, oh, five seconds." Of course, it didn't help any that a few years earlier he'd lost what he and his partner had estimated as a 40-plus-incher at that same bend.

"Couldn't have been the same fish," Tony Zappia told him over drinks. Ron Kolodziej was there, too, and he and I were putting some hardwood on the fire to grill the steaks. "If it was, that fish would be 30 pounds by now. Probably more."

This is a group unaccustomed to finding itself at a loss for words.

Jigs should be dressed for success. A marabou skirt and a supple trailer help. Plastic worms, twister tails, shimmy minnows, and pork strips all make good trailer choices. The more things that wiggle and dance without much movement, the better, although certain trailers work better on certain days, and I really have no answer why. My very tentative conclusions find bare shimmy shads (paddle-tailed rubber minnows) at their best along well-defined weedlines, particularly where the structure goes from weeds to nothing—from 15 feet to, say, 35. If the water is clear, I'm even more inclined to start with them. I much prefer the bigger 5-inch models and use the same color combinations mentioned above for spoons, the difference being that I'm much quicker to turn to the fluorescent yellows and chartreuses.

If the weedline offers less definition, or if you're searching more than targeting, nothing beats the jig and worm. I tie my own jigs, using marabou feathers as hackles. (This is an easy operation, and if you don't tie, explain it to someone who does and he'll be able to whip up a few for you.). I prefer 6- to 7-inch worms with as much wiggle as I can get. In years past I always went with a fluorescent yellow jighead and marabou, and a black worm, the success of which I attributed to its suggestion of the contrasting yellow body and dark bands of a perch. I still use this combo, though not to the extent that I do a white marabou (with Holographic Flashabou tied in) and a fluorescent yellow Culprit worm tail.

Two other jig rigs bear mention, particularly in cold-front situations. Both involve a jig and minnow rigging, not unlike that used by walleye fishermen. One is the minnow and spinner-jig described in chapter 1, which is an ideal way to fish a deep summer point, particularly in the morning or evening when the fish might be a bit more aggressive and holding up on the slope. The minnow and spinner-jig is an excellent combo for probing the slack water behind a point in a river, too. A weighted walleye spinner and minnow can be a good choice if the fish are holding a bit off the structure.

For sharp drop-offs, a jig and minnow can be even better. Some anglers use harnesses, but I much prefer a freshly killed 4-inch minnow rigged on a lightly dressed (or bare) jighead. Bucktail makes a better skirt choice than marabou, as the latter wraps around and, in effect, shrouds the minnow from view. Work this combo like the jig and worm, though the retrieve should be executed more gently. Whereas the jig and worm strike will often feel like pressure, strikes on a minnow-tipped jig will often manifest as a *tap-tap*. Drop the rod tip and strike as hard as your tackle permits.

Toughest summer conditions? I think cold fronts, although some anglers like fishing then. Here's what Joe Bednar, president of Pikemasters says: "After a weather system passes, the first day (at least) afterward is usually characterized by clear skies, and cooler winds out of the north or northwest. This high [barometric] pressure weather often brings the best pike action, including encounters with big pike, when it comes to summer and fall piking. I emphasize this because it goes against the grain of what many of us have been taught. Apparently, pike find cool to cold fronts refreshing during summer and fall (up to the point of turnover, anyway)."

I have taken some very nice fish on the kind of day that Bednar describes, though all in all, I find cold fronts tough. My friend Tony Zappia and I hit such a day once, and the only combination that would draw a hit was a Silver Minnow rigged with a chartreuse Mister Twister cast within inches of the overhanging brush. The pike would grab it on the fall.

I encountered an even more miserable day of pike fishing several summers ago, in August, on the St. Lawrence River. I was fishing with my friend Jim Burr and my son, Brody, who was four at the time. It was drizzly and cold, and by mid-afternoon we had little to show for our efforts save a few rock bass, small (and I mean small) perch, and some sublegal smallmouths. We were blue faced and fished out. Brody asked me what I was going to say in my book about pike fishing in the rain. I started to say, "Not too damn much," but caught myself. "Hmm, I'm not sure."

I'd tried all kinds of jigs and such, even a jig and minnow. Then I looked in the bucket and saw the sucker we'd bought that morning, when hopes were high. It was belly-up, so I did some hacking and took a 4-inch slice off the side, left some skin fluttering, and hooked it to the jighead. "Last chance," I said.

"I'm not even going to ask where that came from," Jim said. I showed him the eviscerated sucker before flipping it overboard. "Okay, just checking."

I began casting, trying to put the jig on a weed edge that went from 15 to 20 feet. I set the hook at some resistance. Weeds. I cleaned up and flipped out again. There was an aliveness this time, a tick, ever so slight. I dropped the rod tip and set the hook hard. There. A pike. I knew it.

I worked the fish to the boat, and it wasn't big at all—even by our puny civilized standards. It might have been 24 inches long. But you know, I've never in my life been so overcome by a toothy overbite. I can see how pro bass anglers kiss fish, though thoughts of a certain Russian ice fisherman quelled that impulse in a hurry. I got the pike to the boat, grabbed it behind the head, and popped out the hook with my pliers.

"Watch this, Brody." I squeezed the fish behind the back fins, and it scooted down to the weedbed, a trail of tiny bubbles following it into the green depths of the St. Lawrence.

*Northern Canada provides spring-like fly fishing conditions all summer long.*

# 12

# Fly Fishing in Depth

Once hatches taper off and trout fishing evaporates beneath the withering sun, flinging a pike streamer around some weedbeds starts sounding like a pretty good way to spend an afternoon. Cool water or not, pike still fit into the angling niche of warm water. But if you want to do battle with pike in classic "northern" fashion, that's where you should head. As far north as you can get.

Northern pike patrol the shallow waters of wilderness Canadian lakes all summer, and they remain quite accessible to fly fishers. Reynolds and Berryman will tell you all you need to know about how to catch them in their book *Pike on the Fly* . They put out an instructive and exciting video, too. Watch it and you'll be ordering 9-weights and Bunny Flies like you're flying out tomorrow.

My interest is different. I spend my summers fishing pike in northern United States and southern Canada. The pike from chapter 11, in other words. Not surprisingly, these fish present fly fishers with the same problems they do casters, drifters, and trollers, but you don't hear much about this side of fly fishing for northerns. As with the "theory" of fishing for pike in general, much of the "theory" of fly fishing for pike comes from the wilderness experience.

This thinking can limit fly-fishing success in spring, but it poses real problems as the season progresses. Summer pike make a much more challenging fly-rod quarry than you'd think. Most days you won't catch very many of them. You have to like trying to figure them out, which I do, although I certainly understand why people might not.

*Summer pike will occasionally take topwater bugs in morning and evening. This wilderness pond is a 10-mild paddle back into New York's Adirondack Mountains.*

Most anglers don't drive a 5-inch streamer on a high-density sinking-tip through a 20 mph wind in order to appreciate fly fishing's delicate, cerebral dimensions.

## DEEP-WATER CHALLENGES

If you want to flog the shallow weeds, you're better off tying on a hair frog and hoping for a largemouth. Any pike still swimming by the middle of July will be doing so in 10 to 15 feet of water at the least, and possibly quite a bit more. A 6- or 7-pounder is a good-sized summer northern, and a really good one for a fly rodder. Bigger fish than that hang in deep water and eat infrequently—not exactly ideal fly-fishing circumstances.

It can take awhile to appreciate the strategic dimension to summer pike fishing. The first idea to get your head around is that pike are opportunists; they don't select for species, but for behavior. I'm repeating this point, I know. But it has always annoyed the living hell out of the fly fisher in me. No way out, either. Northerns are dug in on this one.

Check out this study, completed in 1971, on the forage of pike:

Conditioning appeared to have no effect on food selection by northern pike. Conditioning can be thought of as the training of an organism to feed on a specific food in the presence of a choice of foods. In two experiments in pools, six pike were fed only golden shiners for 65 and 114 days in an attempt to condition them to feed on golden shiners. Then the pike were offered a choice of food, and their diet was compared with that of pike that were offered the same choice of food but had not been fed golden shiners. The percentage of the ration made up of golden shiners was 12 for both groups of pike.

These experiments were replicated with other prey species, by the way. Compare the inclinations of these pike with the selectivity of trout after a weeklong hatch of sulfurs. Like I said, psycho.

As we know, pike do make a selection, even if along a different axis—that is, not on the basis of prey species, but prey behavior, specifically vulnerability. That's a better entry point than the "pick-a-forage" avenue that characterizes other fly-fishing approaches, although I still tie flies that look like different pike foods. I know it doesn't matter to the fish, but on some aesthetic level it does to me. In any case, if you want to catch fish, you're imitating behavior, which presents its own challenges. It's hard to pick the right-colored streamer and make it look alive and vulnerable 25 feet down. You can lose yourself in the intricacies of presentations. Open-water pike fight from the moment you hook them, too. In short, I've come to appreciate fly fishing for pike during the summer. It just took awhile.

At first I tried various streamers with little success. Quick retrieves that worked in the shallows didn't in the depths, because the motion only pulled the fly toward the surface. Matters improved when I gave up trying to imitate perch and alewives and started imitating the summer artificial that I knew worked, namely a jig and worm. That got me focused on color and behavior before I realized what I was doing.

I started with plenty of marabou, a Zonker strip, and enough weight at the head of the fly to bring out some action. In essence, that fly offered a package comparable with the jig and worm. The jig and worm is feather and rubber; my pike flies were feather and fur. In those days I was using a yellow jig and black worm, and I tied the fly the same way. I didn't know about dumbbell eyes, so I weighted the head with lead wire and covered it with yellow fur. Doll eyes cemented on the fur head and white rubber legs in between the winds of hackle provided the final touches. I was ready for a maiden voyage.

My old friend Pete Bellinger had moved to Ogdensburg, New York, an hour or so downriver on the St. Lawrence, and he'd been after me to do some bass fishing. I agreed on the condition that we spend at least two hours of the day prospecting for pike.

It was close to dusk when we slipped into a deep, weedy bay on the downriver side of some old pilings. What a summer pike spot. Deep water of 15 to 20 feet, a half-mile-long weed complex, and protection from the river's currents. Pete anchored on the outside edge of the weeds so that he could fish the current for small-mouths, and I got down to business.

I rigged up with wire leader, 3 feet of 20-pound mono, and fast-sinking line, and began casting to the weeds. I tried various retrieves—short strips, long strips. Nothing. It wasn't until I fell into a retrieve comprised of a series of short, quick strips that a scrawny pike of several pounds followed my fly in, only to turn away at the boat, probably because Pete shouted, "Boo!" as the pike came into view. "Just a baby," he explained.

That little hammer handle gave me hope. I tried combining the free fall and fast strip by letting the fly sink to the bottom, starting it for a few yards with fast strips, then dropping the rod tip and roll casting 10 feet so that the resulting pile of line would let the fly free fall. Once the line came taut, I'd twitch it. That's when I saw a strike. Literally. The line moved about half an inch to the left, just where it entered the water, and I set the hook as quickly as possible. It was like hooking into a cinder block, which made sense because I'd hooked the anchor. We pulled up, extracted my fly from the chain at the head of the anchor, and readjusted our position. "It's only because we're friends, you know," Pete said.

And then another twitch, this time on the first strip after a drop. It felt like a perch bite, a tick, and I struck hard again. This was a fish. A good one. It lunged for the weeds, and I could feel its weight in my arms. I got it started back up. Pete got the net.

"Remember that pike I lost in front of my dad's cottage back in Chaumont Bay?" Pete said.

"I thought you didn't care about pike."

"Watch the anchor rope," Pete said.

Man, I wanted that fish.

## TACKLE AND FLIES

Since then I've played around with various imitations and presentations and tackle. Here's what I've come up with.

Weed cover thins as you drop down to the 15- to 25-foot depths that hold summer pike. There's little worry about keeping fish out of thick tangles at those depths. The concern is achieving a natural presentation.

A 7-weight outfit does the trick, though an 8-weight is probably more in line with what most anglers would want. Pike streamers can be good sized, and you also want to be able to set the hook with authority. Deep-water pike strikes often just feel like weight at the end of the line, by the way. As soon as you feel resistance, you've really got to rear back.

I used to fish a floating line and 20-foot leader in deep water, thinking that would accentuate the drop, but I don't think it makes much of a difference once you get below 12 feet. These days I use a high-density sinking tip and a 5-foot leader of 10-pound test. The reasonably light leader enhances the free-falling flutter that appeals to pike. Either way, you'll want one of the shock leaders described in chapter 9.

As for flies, action matters more than pattern since you're imitating behavior, not species. Big Clouser Minnows can be very effective in deep water, as can the subsurface patterns listed in Reynolds and Berryman. The Barr 'Bou Face is more or less the same fly (without the weighted head and rubber feet) that I tied in my attempt to imitate a jig and worm. Nearly all the fly-fishing catalogs offer pike flies nowadays, and they all work. If there's a problem with the patterns, it lies not in their inability to imitate forage but in the fact that they are designed to be fished in shallow water and come with excessively long tails, which encourage short strikes.

I emphasize the following components in my flies: visible eyes, marabou, flash, and trailing saddle hackles. A healthy splash of red is always in order, too. In general, I use silver flash in clear water, gold in stained. The Marabou Pike Streamer (Pattern 1), noted in chapter 9, works well in summer, too. If there's a difference, it comes in hook size—I prefer the shorter hook (4X as opposed to 8X long) for deep water. Most days the Marabou Pike Streamer is the first one on my line.

Here are some other favorite summer patterns, all of which are pictured in the color plates, with the exception of the Corsair Perch.

**PATTERN 2: JIG AND WORM**

*Hook* - Size 2/0, 2X long.
*Thread* - Monocord.
*Head* - Lead wire. Yellow or chartreuse Lite Brite, dubbed.
*Eyes* - ⅜-ounce red and black dumbbell eyes.
*Hackle* - Fluorescent yellow, chartreuse, and orange marabou mixed with Holographic Flashabou.
*Tail* - Black, red, orange, yellow, or chartreuse Zonker strip (with corresponding Flashabou).

*Instructions:*

1. Tie and glue (CA) dumbbell eyes to the top of the hook (so that the hook rides upright). Figure-eight lead wire around the eyes.
2. For the tail, tie in the Zonker strip and Flashabou.
3. Wind marabou hackles, securing the holographic tinsel so that it marries with the marabou. It may help to pinch flat the stem of the marabou hackles before securing them to the hook.
4. Finish the head with dubbed Lite Brite.

*Notes:* Although black has never been one of my favorite pike colors, this pattern tied with a black Zonker strip has worked very well for me—perhaps because it offers a strong color contrast with the lighter marabou. This design is very close to the Barr 'Bou Face, included in Reynolds and Berryman, the differences being the contrasting hackle and tail, the Flashabou married with hackled marabou, and the weight at the head.

## SUMMER PRESENTATIONS

Occasionally, you'll find summer pike in shallow water, and these spots are always worth a shot. Just two years ago my friend Stan Warner and I found ourselves motoring out of a Lake Champlain boat launch at dawn. There was a whisper of wind from the south, but something didn't feel right. I realized what it was as light came creeping down the creek. The water. There was more of it; current, too. And the color seemed dark, chocolate brown, to be precise. Turns out it had rained heavily for two days, but we'd had no idea, having driven up in the dark from Massachusetts. Out in the bay the water was more of the same.

"Do you want to even bother?" I asked.

"Well, we're here." Which is a pretty typical Stan response that in retrospect I am most thankful for. We were that close to not fishing.

We motored through the muddy water and found that the wind was blowing against the flow of the creek as it plumed into the bay. This was a shallow bay, 12 feet tops. The convergence of wind-pushed clear water and current-driven muddy water

## PATTERN 3: MARABOU MATUKA

*Hook* - 1/0, 4X long.
*Thread* - Brown.
*Head* - Brown.
*Eyes* - Yellow and black (stick-on).
*Wings* - Marabou and Flashabou.
*Body* - Lead wire underbody. Dubbed white rabbit and Lite Brite.
*Throat* - Red Sparkle Floss.

### Instructions:

1. Wrap the underbody with lead wire and cement.
2. Tie in the marabou feathers, Matuka-style. Add Flashabou—one strand for each clump.
3. Dub the body, separating the wing section, from front to rear and then from rear to front. Keep the body short to prevent the marabou from wrapping around the hook on the cast. Wrap red Sparkle Floss or thread for the gills. Cement and paint the head.

*Notes:* This is my favorite open-water pattern, and it's a good fly for slow days. I weight the body quite heavily to generate a sharp drop, and I tie the Matuka wing with a lot of white marabou and silver Flashabou to suggest the silvery struggles of an alewife. Luhr-Jensen makes Flashabou called Lure Flash, which comes in all shades (even chartreuse) if you want to put a fine point on the marriage of color and flash. Some anglers may hesitate at the thought of spending up to an hour tying a fly that a pike can rip apart in 10 seconds. But these streamers are actually surprisingly durable when tied Matuka-style. Anyway, I really enjoy watching my friends worry about the well-being of my streamer flies.

## PATTERN 4: SPARKLE GRUB

*Hook* - Size 1/0, 4X long.
*Thread* - Monocord.
*Head* - Lead wire. Chartreuse Estaz.
*Eyes* - ¼-ounce red and black dumbbell eyes.
*Body* - Chartreuse Estaz.
*Tail* - Chartreuse marabou with corresponding Flashabou.

### Instructions:

1. Tie dumbbell eyes to the top of the hook (so that the hook rides up-right). Use CA glue to secure the eyes. Figure-eight the lead wire, wrapping it halfway down the shank of the hook.
2. Tie in the marabou and Flashabou tail.
3. Tie in and wind the Estaz body.

*Notes:* The Sparkle Grub is a pattern I use for smallmouth bass, but in longer sizes it works well for northerns, too. This fly is at its best when pitched tight to a weedline or other obstruction. It is the most out-of-the-closet jig in my pike-fly selection, but it works when others don't, so I include it. Fire Tiger is a good color, too.

## PATTERN 5: CORSAIR STREAMER (PERCH)

*Hook:* 1/0 6X long.
*Thread:* Olive.
*Head:* Silver embossed Corsair.
*Eyes:* Gold stick-ons, with black center.
*Gills:* Fire red thread.
*Hackle:* Olive and orange marabou.
*Body:* Yellow Lite Brite.
*Wing:* Four grizzly saddle hackles dyed yellow and olive, and yellow and olive Flashabou; topped with 8 to 10 strands of peacock swords and green Krystal Flash.

*Instructions:*

1. Wrap the underbody with heavy lead wire, with an extra layer near the head.
2. Dub the body with yellow Lite Brite.
3. Tie in the saddle hackles, splayed, at the halfway point in the body. Continue dubbing with Lite Brite for ¼ inch in front of hackles.
4. Wrap marabou hackles in the following order, from back to front: olive, then yellow, then orange. Hackle should be wrapped to within ¹⁄₁₆ inch of the eye of the hook.
5. Tie in the Flashabou, Krystal Flash, and peacock swords on top.
6. Slip a ⅝-inch piece of Corsair over the eye of the hook and push it back over the wing topping material and hackle. Tie it down first at the nose with olive thread; then tie on fire red thread for gills (over the Corsair). Wrap several times and tie off. This secures the stacked appearance of the "underhead," which will show through the Corsair: The throat should be the yellow marabou, the top, the peacock sword.
7. Cement the head thoroughly, first with vinyl cement. Add eyes while the cement is tacky. Let dry and add two coats (to the entire head) of gloss cement.

*Notes:* Okay. So here's the mandatory perch imitation. Every pike fisherman has several such lures or flies in his box. I've never had much luck with them—lure, plug, or fly. I think they catch more fishermen than fish, although I actually did catch a pike on this pattern last summer.

A brainchild of Jack Gartside, Corsair gives a nice scaled effect to the head, and I've used the same tying technique with other streamers, particularly white, blue, and chartreuse. I caught a number of pike on a white and silver Corsair Streamer this past summer. This pattern works well when summer pike are up on shoals in 6 to 10 feet of water or so and the situation calls for a moderately deep horizontal retrieve.

created a distinct line, leaving four fifths of the bay mud. A crescent of clear water remained along its edge.

"I hear that mudlines can be good," Stan said.

"You've been watching too many fishing shows," I said.

## PATTERN 6: LITTLE PIKE

*Hook:* 1/0 6X long.
*Thread:* Olive.
*Head:* Olive-brown bucktail, cemented into a "pike" shape.
*Eyes:* Orange stick-ons, with light dumbbells.
*Hackle:* Olive and brown speckled marabou.
*Wing:* Four grizzly saddle hackles dyed yellow and olive; and yellow, olive, and gold Flashabou.

*Instructions:*

1. Tie in the saddle hackles, splayed, along with the Flashabou.
2. Wrap the marabou hackles and Flashabou. The hackle should be wrapped to within ¾ inch of the hook eye.
3. Tie in the eyes on the top of the hook. Make sure the dumbbells are light in weight so as to keep the fly running properly.
4. Tie in the bucktail at the nose, secure on the back of the eyes, and cement.
5. Clip the bottom of the marabou hackle.

*Notes:* This pattern is really a permutation of Dick Stewart's ingenious Li'l Pickerel, which is described in *Bass Flies*. I can't imagine a time when pike would take this fly and not some others, but I enjoy fishing this pattern anyway. For the record, I work it on a sinking-tip in 5 to 10 feet of water, early in the morning.

Stan turned to answer and lost a fish. But he hooked a smallmouth bass on his next cast, while a pike chased my streamer to the boat and caught it as my leader was in the guides. It was like a midnight madness sale. Over the next eight hours we caught fish after fish. Clouds of minnows swarmed about the strip of clear water. A biologist later explained that with no oxygen in the mud, the baitfish had to enter the shrinking crescent of clear water, where the pike, smallmouths, and largemouths were waiting. At one point Stan hooked about a 10-pound northern on a Rapala and lost it because a pike a third its size tried to take away the plug and bit through his line instead. I cast my streamer and caught the smaller pike, so at least everybody got lunch.

But basing fishing strategies on biblical rains is not exactly what you'd call playing the percentages. These sorts of days represent real exceptions. Most pike spend their summers eying schools of forage fish that move along a deep weedline. They look for the bait they can catch, which usually means a solitary minnow. Their selectivity organizes around this assessment. As research on spottail shiners (cited in chapter 4) indicates, the shiners disperse more at low light. Other forage shows similar tendencies. It would certainly follow that pike find the hunting best when their prey are most vulnerable (scattered and unable to use their mirrorlike sides to hide in the bright light), but the overall visibility is still good. So cloudy conditions may help. Many pike anglers believe that midmorning (from 8 to 11 A.M.) and late afternoon and evening (from 3 to 8 P.M.) are the best times to fish, and that has been my experience, too—particularly when I'm summer fly fishing and need all the help I can get.

Regardless of time of day, fishing begins with finding a deep structure that might draw a feeding pike. Summer pike may move on top of a weedy shoal during low light or as a front approaches, but otherwise they remain on the deep-water edge, locating down on the weedline, waiting for the prey to come to them. As for which fly pattern gets the starting nod, I select whatever comes closest to the most effective spoon, plug, or jig in the particular body of water I'm fishing. In terms of color, white initially gets the go-ahead, as I believe it signals vulnerability. And as the above fly patterns suggest, I am a big believer in the combination of weight and marabou. Flies dressed accordingly can be fished slowly with a good deal of action.

Thus, too, the success of the light-tackle, cast-and-flutter technique with weighted streamers that in effect involves a deeper, heavier, slower version of spring retrieves. Consistent with their interest in struggling forage fish, pike seem to prefer streamers with a swim-stop-drop motion. One particular retrieve worth trying is the *exaggerated* swim-stop-drop. This involves hurrying the streamer in quick strips, then feeding slack line, then stripping quickly again, and so forth. The more slack you can feed, the better, as in part you're imitating a baitfish heading for the bottom.

The basic presentation, then, involves casting parallel to the edge of the weedbed and retrieving back with a stop-and-drop so that the streamer falls in plain view of whatever is hiding in the weeds. I usually try to drift along a weed edge and continue to cast toward the vegetation. The outside edge, where water drops down to 20 feet, comprises the prime area—particularly in midlake or midriver situations. Shallower weedlines that fall from 3 or 4 feet and very thick weeds to 10 feet and thin weeds can be good spots on cloudy days or just before a storm.

It's easier to fish downdrift, but updrift holds overlooked opportunities. For one thing, your fly spends more time on a free fall or dive, diving being a common predator-avoidance behavior for pike prey and hence a trigger for summer pike. You want a true free fall—a drag-free fall, in effect. Try finishing it off with twitches of life, and try also to avoid the easy casting behind the boat or with the wind, and turn around and face updrift, upwind, or upcurrent. Trout anglers will recognize this advice as the timeworn "advantage of fishing upstream," which has colored the pages of wet-fly and nymph-fishing treatises since they started putting eyes on hooks. It might sound misplaced in a discussion of pike strategies, but fly fishing northerns in summer means a new set of rules.

As earlier in the year, drifting and trolling streamers can be a very good strategy, particularly on a long weedline, and particularly if you hit a stretch of hot weather late in summer. I remember fishing a Lake Ontario bay one fiercely hot day in a fiercely hot week during a fiercely hot August. We were on Lee Ellsworth's boat—Scott Johnson, Steve Charles, Marcel Rocheleau, Lee, and I. A herd of us, in other words, and by noon we were snorting and panting like a boatload of livestock. We decided to troll, as we were near the weedy drop-off that nearly always gave Lee and me a pike or two. "If nothing else," Lee said, "we'll get a breeze."

One of the keys to trolling is to get the speed that works for various lures. To get crankbaits to run at the 10- to 15-foot range, you need to bounce right along; to get spoons to run properly at that depth, you need to back off a bit. Streamer flies can be worked at a variety of speeds, and that's a good thing, because we intended to pull crankbaits, except for Marcel, who wanted to troll streamers. We started off, sprouting rods and lines, the only float in our own parade.

We hadn't gone 20 yards when Scott hooked a pike, a nice one that ran back toward the weeds.

"Watch your line, Marcie," Lee said.

Marcel started cranking in his streamer. Then his rod bowed deeply, too. "Fish on!"

Lee, Steve, and I watched the circus as Scott and Marcel battled their pike at the back of the boat. You could feel the wind coming up, fluky here inside the bay as it swirled over the protection of the land, and Lee said to no one in particular, "You know, this could be really good."

He was right, as it turned out. The afternoon fishing blew up as the wind gusted with the approaching front, but we were able to remain in the lee of the shore. We caught some 15 pike, lost as many, and Marcel's white marabou streamer was by far the dominant artificial. He fished it on a fast-sinking line, with four big split shot strung along the leader.

Later that night, after a line of thunderstorms had come crashing through, we returned to clean out the boat and stow gear. The air had cleared, and a northwest wind gave the little bay a new feel. Not fall yet, but you knew what was coming. The conversation turned to the pike, how they took that day. As Lee noted, the pike in this bay loved a change of pace, whether slowing or speeding. Indeed, many of Marcel's strikes came as the boat was turning, which caused the fly to accelerate. The speed triggered the strike.

So there is a complexity to pike fishing. Less the pattern-based selectivity that we associate with trout fishing or the situation-based selectivity we associate with smallmouth bass, it has to do with questions such as, "Do I have the energy to try to catch that thing, and can I catch it if I try?" What if the pike watched a parade of forage swim by, when one individual suddenly rose up and veered off on its own, as if panicking and choosing an ineffective prey avoidance maneuver? The better decision would have been to dive, which is what the school of crankbaits did when the boat speeded up. Marcel's fly, perhaps, became the young gazelle that runs away from the herd. And we know what happens to him.

So, yes, great northern pike are selective, but they stick to their own criteria when making up their minds. And somehow that fits pike perfectly. They just never manage to stay inside the lines.

# PART IV

## Fall

# 13

# The Pike in Fall

Surface temperatures reach the 80s in many pike lakes and rivers in early August, but by the end of the month they start heading in the other direction. Crisp nights cool the water's surface, and temps drop into the 70s. In F. Scott Fitzgerald's *The Great Gatsby,* Jordan Baker observed that "life starts all over again when it gets crisp in the fall." Baker was referring to the wealthy who summered in the Hamptons, but she may as well have been speaking of northern pike, which likewise while away the warm months in a cool vacation home.

Seasonal changes influence fish long before the season in question is upon us. Pike begin staging for spawn while we're worrying about where to set tip-ups. So it is that fall pike fishing begins in what we would call late summer, maybe on the kind of oppressively humid afternoon that gave rise to Jordan Baker's observation in the first place.

I'm generally of two minds regarding this time of year. My summer vacation from teaching is evaporating like a rain puddle on cement, but the fishing on the St. Lawrence River gets better every day. And you can definitely catch some big pike during this transitional time in late August and early September. Spinnerbaits, in-line bucktail spinners, and crankbaits are all top producers. Brisk horizontal presentations make good choices for trolling or casting over deep, weedy flats and along weedlines. Jigging with spoons and rubber can be effective off points, along drop-offs, and in deep coves. In many ways this period doesn't represent a change in pike location so much as a change in pike mood. Vacation is over.

*Summer is a time for fun fishing.*

## SEE YOU IN SEPTEMBER

I'm not the first person to happen on this idea, of course. Back in August 1939, as the world waited for World War II, a man named Peter Dubuc was just getting started with his fall pike fishing in the southern Adirondacks of New York State. His favorite spot was Great Sacandaga Lake, actually a reservoir that had been in existence but 10 years. Dubuc owned a camp on Sacandaga, and he and his wife fished it frequently.

As Dubuc later noted, you could feel things changing in late summer. And he was a man with a plan, as he explained the next spring in *Field & Stream:*

> Some bright August morning when the water is down to the proper level, we start
> looking over the old stump beds for pike. . . . At 5:30 in the morning of September
> 3 on our last summer's vacation we were on our way to a stump field at the mouth
> of Han's Creek. A half hour later we were on the spot and I had a Heddon Crazy
> Crawler rigged with an 18 inch bronze leader and a small clinch sinker to take the

Crawler down just a little. The sun came up nice and hot, to my liking, as the morning was cool.

An hour after I started casting I dropped the Crazy Crawler right alongside an old stump protruding above the surface—and a depth bomb went off. It wasn't long before I knew that I had something real, but it was a long time before I subdued him. My wife claims that she timed it an hour and a half. . . . Toward the end of the battle the big fellow fouled the line on a stump, and, being pretty desperate by then, I got right out of the boat and into the water to work that line free. By the time I got back in the boat I don't know who was more tired, the fish or me, but it wasn't long before I brought him within reach of the gaff.

Now this is where I would like to discount a lot of people's theories about fishing at midday. We stuck it out, casting in the same spot until afternoon. It was well past one o'clock when, very near the same spot on a fast retrieve, I had another hard strike and had to go through the same thing all over again. When we had this one in the boat, we called it a day and started for camp. Upon weighing our catch we found that we had one weighing 35 pounds 6 ounces and another weighing 32 pounds 9 ounces.

The story comes to us like so much else of pike legend: a famous plug, a man-made lake on the edge of wilderness, a fish behaving like it could, but not like it should. All on the day the Blitzkrieg roared through Europe and forever changed the world.

Fall fishing apparently agreed with Dubuc. The next year, on September 15, he caught an even bigger pike in the same reservoir, one that weighed 46 pounds, 2 ounces, to this day the North American record. My friend Ron Kolodziej, a writer who lives near the Sacandaga, has researched this pike and reports the following in a recent *New York Sportsman* article:

Accounts vary somewhat and run the gamut from Dubuc catching his big pike on a fly to finding the fish near death on the surface with a smaller pike stuck in its throat. . . . In all likelihood, Dubuc was casting plugs (probably a Pikie Minnow) from a boat in the Benedict Bay area of the lake when the big pike hit his lure in a stumpy near-shore area only a few feet deep. . . . Dubuc's 12-pound test line, two feet of copper leader and steel casting rod held fast. After a 55 minute struggle . . . Dubuc was able to haul the monster aboard, without the benefit of a net. . . .

While photos of the fish are said to exist I have not been able to find any, even in the archives of several area newspapers. What happened to the fish? Not wishing to pay the going rate of a dollar an inch to have it mounted, Dubuc brought it home and ate it.

## FALL STRATEGIES

If you were to fish Sacandaga in mid-September these days, you'd be best off trying deeper water. In most big bodies of water pike hold at depths of 15 to 35 feet during August, and move into the 5- to 15-foot range during September. Northerns inhabiting shallow flows, rivers, and smaller lakes and ponds don't shift depths like their big-water kin, but they do become more active during the fall. Sometimes they move into very shallow waters; other times they hide in offshore weedbeds. River pike move out of the deepest pools and assume feeding stations along weedy shores with slack current or near the entrance to brushy coves.

Yes, pike spend more time in shallower water now, but their presence is nothing to take to the bank. Some pike delay coming into the shallows. Some of the smaller adults may never have left; some of the bigger fish never come in at all.

Pike do feed more aggressively in the cool weather. Studies show fall northerns to have fewer empty stomachs than summer pike. For the angler, however, there's no sure thing with feeding, any more than there is with location. Joe Bednar, president of Pikemasters, writes the following about temperatures and fall pike in a recent edition of the organization's newsletter, *Waterwolves:* "Give me the first day after a cold front in the fall, provided the lake hasn't turned over . . . the pattern holds up well through water temps in the sixty degree range then there will be a slump when the water falls through the upper fifty degree range (turnover)." Turnover occurs when the surface waters cool quickly, become heavier than the warmer water below, and the lake, or section thereof, inverts. The fishing dies until the weather settles, the water clarifies, and the temperatures stabilize. In fact, as Bednar notes, "The pattern re-emerges and fishing is good again from about 55 degrees down to about 50, then it gets tough (in my opinion). For what it's worth I encounter as many as 75% of my best pike each year (pike in the mid thirty inch range and up which are very rare in southern Michigan) in just the 4–6 week period from mid September through mid to late October."

Whether they are on the prowl or not, fall pike are no pushovers, and the best strategy for fishing them, no gimme. Working above and beside weedbeds is a good approach on Indian summer days or just before fronts move in. This approach has spinnerbait written all over it, because you can adjust to various situations. You can pump them over the top of weeds or let them drop along the outside edges and start them in slowly, a deadly strategy for chilly fall mornings.

Some days fall pike seem to want a "realistic" shape and swimming action, which calls for a plug of some sort. The same fishing patterns used in summer can be employed effectively on the outsides of weeds in fall, with a Bagley's Shad or C. C. Rattlin' Shad. The Mann's Minus One, which will work in water of a foot or less, makes a good choice for working over the weeds, though you may want to replace the back treble with a bigger-sized hook. At times northerns appear more tentative, almost muskielike in their demeanor. You might try a muskie-sized jerkbait or the Rattlin' Rogue, which will run at depths of 2 to 10 feet (depending on the model) as you twitch it in. The blue, white, and silver is a good fall choice in bigger lakes and rivers where fall pike feed on ciscoes, alewives, and other pelagic forage.

Rapala jerkbaits make good choices, and so do bigger-model Floating Rapalas and Rebels, in part because they fish well in the 3- to 6-foot depths. These plugs also give the pike a good look at a big forage. Fall is definitely the time to try that huge plug somebody gave you as a gag gift.

Trolling on the edges of the weedbeds and drop-offs produces some good pike, too. In fact, if there's such a thing as a traditional fall strategy, it is just this—puttering along the shorelines and underwater shelves. Plugs, including old-timers like the Pikie Minnow, still work, as do spoons and crankbaits. If anything, trolling lets you cover territory, important since locating fall pike can be the most challenging part of fishing them. In the end there's no such thing as a fall pike strategy, per se, however. Big is better, and spinnerbaits, big in-line spinners, crankbaits, jerkbaits, and streamer flies all represent reasonable starting points. As for color, I fish white quite a bit, but I'm more inclined to the oranges, browns, and yellows than during spring. It must be the leaf peeper in me.

With the cold water of November, pike revert to pre-spawn feeding behavior, though in deeper water than in spring. Minnows, fished live, or dead on a jighead, represent the best choice. I've heard of anglers catching northerns on small spoons flutter fished in deep water, but I have never caught a November pike that way myself.

Fall fishing is challenging. The pike have been in the ring all season, leaving more to fall lure choice than simply matching presentation to structure and depth. There's also the matter of imitating a believable prey behavior and, perhaps more important, a believable prey behavior that appeals to the mood of the pike. Sometimes these choices revolve around lure speed, sometimes action, sometimes both.

Our inclination as anglers is nearly always to change color when the fish don't bite—or, perhaps even more humanly, to change to another favorite lure, all the while changing location. That's what I do, too. But the more you can also make lure changes along the continuum of pike mood (inactive, indifferent, sluggish, active, and aggressive, respectively), the better your chances become—at any time of year, really.

How do these choices play out? Some sort of dead bait, rigged on a jig or spinner-jig, would be a reasonable selection for inactive pike. The same lure might work for an indifferent fish, though so could a frisky live bait. A dropping artificial,

*This fall northern took a start and stop spinnerbait on the edge of an offshore shoal.*

such as a jig and rubber or a stop-and-start spinnerbait, perhaps a jerkbait, might be the ticket for sluggish pike. For active fish, you might start with brisk horizontal presentations—spinners and spinnerbaits, spoons, crankbaits, even buzzbaits. For aggressive fish, just be sure your fingers are inside the canoe.

## THE PIKE IN OUR FUTURE, THE PIKE IN OUR PAST

Because I am back teaching in New England during the fall, much of my pike fishing centers upon Lake Champlain. My most recent fall trip, on the last weekend of September, gets started on Saturday at six in the morning, with my little boy, Brody, along for the adventure. We are due in Swanton, Vermont, at 10 A.M., where we'll meet up with some friends and fish Missisquoi Bay for the last trip of the season. The interstate is clogged with leaf peepers heading north for the glorious foliage. Brody's seven and not at a loss for questions. I dodge Volvos.

"Dad, what is the biggest pike anybody ever caught?"

"I don't know about the world, but the biggest pike ever caught in America or Canada came from the Sacandaga Reservoir in New York."

"Where's that?"

"About 100 miles that way," and I point across the mountains.

"What did the guy catch the pike on?"

"A Pikie Minnow, probably."

"I've never caught a pike on a lure," Brody says.

"Try a white spinnerbait," I say. "I think you've got one in your tackle box."

He lifts the tackle box on his lap. We go through all the lures, which are the best for pike, which are the best for big pike, which are best in Lake Champlain, which are best now. Then he closes the box, puts it in the backseat, and keeps a white spinnerbait to look at. "I want to catch a pike on a lure," he says and falls asleep, spinnerbait on his lap. I reach over, pick it up, and drop it in my shirt pocket. At his age, I wanted to catch one on a spear.

Ahead of me Vermont's fiery mountain spine stretches north, poking through the morning mist. The weather looks good, though with fall fishing, you never know. I worry that the water hasn't had a chance to cool, then I recall the last two cool nights and fret that maybe it has become *too* cool. Maybe the bay just turned over. Maybe the water's muddy. Maybe, maybe, maybe.

I always get a kick out of nonanglers observing that fishing must be a great way to relax. I usually tell them to check out *Moby Dick* and the mellow Captain Ahab.

The I-89 traffic thins out north of Burlington, Vermont's biggest city. The foliage is "better" in the central part of state, where the mountains dominate the landscape. Up here it is closer to the lake plain, and partway between Burlington and Swanton the interstate rises above the vista west, revealing the entire shape of northern Lake Champlain with dots of green speckling the distant blue waters, and granite-faced Adirondacks with their shaggy manes of reds and yellows. The mountains look old, standing in the background. The topography flattens out to the north, courtesy of the mighty St. Lawrence River Valley, foreshadowing the lay of the land in Great Lakes country to the west. The high country of Vermont occupies the easternmost edge of the pike's indigenous North American range, one that stretches from here to the Rockies and as far north as humans can travel. The view is most grand.

It is quite possible, if not likely, that the first European encounter with a North American pike occurred here in Champlain. Today, 350 years later, we're still encountering them, ice fishing them in winter, shooting them in spring, fishing for them the rest of the year. *Multiuse* is a current buzzword in resource management, and I guess you won't find a more multiuse fish than these Champlain pike. Good news for tourism on Champlain, bad news for our toothy friends. In many ways, of course, Champlain pike are simply a microcosm of pike everywhere in the northern United States and southern Canada. If anything, their average size is holding up better than with the heavily ice-fished pike in the northern Midwest.

I can't help thinking that we're at a crossroads in the history of these pike populations as they continue to sustain significant, year-round pressure. But in many ways that's simply business as usual for northern pike. I mean, we have them up there in the Great North, where they oblige us by putting the fishing in our wilderness. They also manage to slip some wilderness in our everyday fishing, and we like them—a few of them, anyway—down here, too. That's a lot to expect from a gamefish, if you ask me, and I'm pretty impressed with how well they pull off these incongruous roles. And they do it with flair, I might add, for few gamefish so embody the "spectacle," whether in wilderness or civilization.

I remember one September afternoon fishing with my friend Stan Warner in Lac Deux Montagnes, an auspicious body of water resulting from the marriage of the Ottawa River with the St. Lawrence. My dad was a trout fisherman, so I was raised to do my fishing in secret, but Stan has no such compunctions. As it turns out, Stan's favorite hole was right below the Route 40 bridge, one of the main arteries leading into Montreal.

"I like this spot," he said over the engine noise on the way out. "It's got heavy weed growth, which we're going over right now. Then we'll hit irregular pockets of weeds in 4- to 10-foot flats, which is where the fish are. The flats fall off into 20 to 30 feet, and that gives the big pike some deep water."

Stan is a start-shallow-and-work-deep kind of guy, so we floated through the 2- to 3-foot depths. He cast a Fire Tiger Mann's Minus One in shallow weeds, while I worked an orange and black spinnerbait with a fluorescent yellow worm trailer.

"There's one!" Stan said, and I turned to see him into a very nice fish that burned line and then jumped. We both yelled, "Muskie," which we'll take anytime as long as we don't have to look stoic and troll for them. But the fight ended almost immediately when the fish wrapped the line around a snag and pulled free.

We fished the shallows furiously after that, but without much luck until midafternoon, when we started to catch a few pike. Meanwhile, over our heads, the traffic on Route 40 had come to a standstill. Motorists were out of the cars, leaning on the rails, smoking, watching us.

Stan landed a small pike, and someone applauded as he held it up for them to see. "This is as close as I'll ever get to fishing on TV," he laughed.

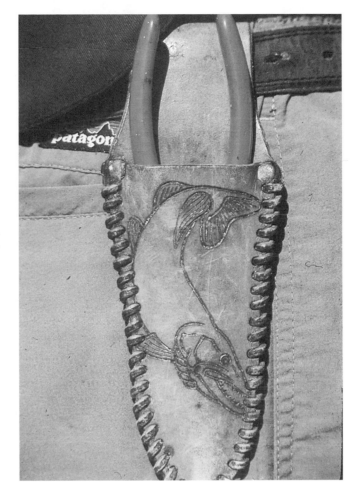

*Fall means dreaming the big one. Be prepared.*

I continued to chuck the spinnerbait and trailer. The fluorescent yellow worm looked eerie against the dark brown background as it came to the boat. Then the pike was there. Right behind the trailer, just there in 2 feet of water. And gone in a swirl.

"Oh my God. Damn!" I said. "You wouldn't believe the size of the pike that just followed my lure." I flipped out to where it had vanished, but nothing.

"How big?"

"I don't know. Big." Then I remembered the traffic jam overhead. Witnesses!

"Hey," I yelled up to the guys leaning on the railing. "Did you guys see that fish? *Pêche?*"

Three nodded and one, bless his soul, held his hands apart in the universal language for big fish. *"Brochet!"* he called down.

"C'mon," I yelled.

*"Grand brochet!"* he replied, as his buddies laughed. And he gave me another 6 to 8 inches. That was better. Metric system, you know.

When I exit from I-89 at Swanton, it's 10 A.M. and I am actually on time. Shawn and his boat greet us at the launch. Marcel and Scott are already out on the bay.

"Let's go fishing," I say to Brody as we roll into the parking lot.

"Huh, we're here, already?" He's one of those kids who wakes up with eyes wide open, like he's embarrassed to admit he was really sleeping. He goes on the offensive as we shake hands with Shawn.

"Where's my spinnerbait?" he asks. I tap my shirt pocket.

And he ends up giving it a good workout on Missisquoi Bay, getting two small northerns by early afternoon, but not the 2-footer he wants. The wind blows from the southwest, but our side of the bay enjoys a lee and the reef becomes choppy but fishable. The fishing picks up. Marcel and Scott take some pike in the 26- to 28-inch range. Shawn fishes flies and finds a streamer presentation that works—wind drifting, with a big white marabou. He casts out from the boat, lets the fly swing into the drift, then twitches it, drops it back 4 or 5 feet, twitches it again. The pike go for it, and he hooks several good ones, including one over 30 inches. I nail a decent fish on a white spinnerbait and trailer. The trick is to stop and start the retrieve; most fish take just as the retrieve begins. I put a trailer on Brody's spinnerbait, tell him about the stop-and-start trick. I have to keep an eye on him because we're drifting through 2-footers and he's winging that spinnerbait out there with both hands.

Then right at the boat there's a swirl and splash, Brody's pole bends into the water. He jams the rod butt in his life jacket, and just as suddenly the line swings free along with the spinnerbait, skirt torn and rubber worm gone, dangling like a bit of ruined jewelry. Brody looks at it, eyes the size of bobbers.

"That was a big one!" Shawn says. "I saw it. Bigger than what your dad got, bigger than the ones Scott and Marcel caught." Shawn's good in these situations.

"As big as the one you caught?"

"Well, let's not get carried away." Even Brody smiles.

We try some more, but the pike don't bite. Brody wants the big pike, we hope along with him. His casting pace picks up. I can certainly relate to his desire, which is palpable as the shadows grow. But the pike doesn't happen.

Like any other fish, northern pike can break your heart. And to tell you the truth, that would be enough to keep me casting for them. But they go one better and do it violently, at close range; you'd swear it's personal.

And I like it that way. When I hook a pike I want to see in its eyes that it knows it's caught, an impulse I trace to early years of feverish casting with one of my uncle Frank's Pikie Minnows, hoping that just one time a great northern would materialize out of the tannic water and crunch down on my lure. At the time I was oblivious to the slim nature of my chances for success, and my uncle had the good sense and grace not to tell me. I learned, strangely, from this gap between not catching yet still knowing that the pike were there. I came to desire pike and *fish* for them, and I think how less interesting pike must be if they enter your awareness as a fish that strikes your lure when you're trying for something else or, as a fish that is simply flown to and caught.

Their pursuit has always filled me with wonder, and for that reason I am most grateful—to anglers I've learned from, friends and family I've fished with, waters I've visited, adventures I've envied, books I've read, tales I've heard, lies I've traded. And for the spirit they have brought to the chase, I want to be sure and extend some gratitude to the great northerns themselves. By my calculations, they've got some coming.

# Selected Bibliography

**Apfelbaum, Ben, Eli Gottlieb, and Steven Michaan.** *Beneath the Ice: The Art of the Spearfishing Decoy.* New York: E. P. Dutton, 1990. Pike, suckers, trout, and perch, probably in that order, are the most popular subjects—but by no means the only ones. Page 79, for instance, shows a wooden crayfish, a frog, a mouse, and a beaver, the latter with a minnow in its mouth. One wonders what on earth this fellow hoped to spear.

**Bailey, John, and Martyn Page.** *Pike: The Predator Becomes the Prey.* Ramsbury, U.K.: The Crowood Press, Ltd., 1985. An in-depth look at British pike fishing, organized by habitat. Best methods for various kinds of waters.

**Bergh, Kit.** *Northern Pike Fishing.* Minneapolis: Dillon Press, 1975. Simply the best book written on North American pike fishing. Bergh is far ahead of his time. Includes interviews with Tom McNally on streamers and Patty Tenny on spoons, respectively. Lucid writing and a real respect for pike and people who fish them.

**Bergman, Ray.** *Just Fishing.* New York: Penn Publishing, 1933. Classic writing on the state of pike fishing in the first four decades of the 20th century.

**Beyerle, George B.** "A Study of Two Northern Pike–Bluegill Populations." *Transactions of the American Fisheries Society* 100 (1971): 69–73. Pike have a difficult time foraging on bluegills, preferring tadpoles in some circumstances.

**Beyerle, George B., and John E. Williams.** "Some Observations of Food Selectivity by Northern Pike in Aquaria." *Transactions of the American Fisheries Society* 97 (1968): 28–31. A fascinating and important look at how pike select forage.

**Beukema, J. J.** "Acquired Hook-Avoidance in the Pike *Esox Lucius L.* Fished with Artificial and Natural Baits." *Journal of Fisheries Biology* 2 (1970): 155–160. A fascinating study of how pike wise up to spinners, but not to live bait.

**Brown, Mick.** *Pike Fishing: The Practice and the Passion.* Ramsbury, U.K.: The Crowood Press, Ltd., 1993. A seasonal approach to catching the big ones in British waters. Excellent detail.

**Bry, Christian, Edgar Basset, Xavier Rognon, and Francois Bonamy.** "Analysis of Sibling Cannibalism among Pike, *Esox Lucius,* Juveniles Reared under Semi-Natural Conditions." *Environmental Biology of Fishes* 35 (1992): 75–84. Overview of young pike cannibalism and comparison with other species.

**Buller, Fred.** *Pike and the Pike Angler.* London: Stanley Paul, 1981. Beautifully written, all-about-pike book that future writers can only hope to approximate.

**Casselman, John M., and Cheryl A. Lewis.** "Habitat Requirements of Northern Pike, *Esox Lucius.*" *Canadian Journal of Fisheries and Aquatic Sciences.* 53 (Suppl. 1) (1996): 161–174. Importance of spring nurseries in northern pike populations.

**Chapman, Colin A., and W. C. Mackay.** "Direct Observation of Habitat Utilization by Northern Pike." *Copeia* 1 (1984): 256–258. An excellent report on how pike disperse and how cannibalism may play a part in this process.

———. "Versatility in Habitat Use by a Top Aquatic Predator, *Esox Lucius, L.*" *Journal of Fisheries Biology* 25 (1984): 109–115. Shows that pike use offshore habitat on windy days, onshore habitats on calm days, regardless of sun. Pike appear as using a wide range of habitat. Suggests that size may explain capacity for ranging.

**Chapman, Laura J., and William C. Mackay.** "Ecological Correlates of Feeding Flexibility in Northern Pike, *Esox Lucius.*" *Journal of Freshwater Ecology* 5, 3 (June 1990): 313–322. More evidence for seasonal variation of prey.

**Cook, Mark F., and Eric P. Bergersen.** "Movements, Habitat Selection, and Activity Periods of Northern Pike in Eleven Mile Reservoir, Colorado." *Transactions of the American Fisheries Society* 117 (1988): 495–502. An interesting study that emphasized pike's use of weeds and, importantly, how wind and sun influence pike location.

**Craig, John F., ed.** *Pike: Biology and Exploitation.* London: Chapman and Hall, 1996. Important information on predation and dependence on vegetation throughout the life cycle. See, in particular, material on cannibalism.

**Crossman, E. J., and J. M. Casselman.** *An Annotated Bibliography of the Pike,* Esox lucius *(Osteichthyes: Salmoniformes).* Toronto: Royal Ontario Museum Publications in Life Sciences, 1987. A 334-page annotated bibliography on pike. A very helpful resource.

**Diana, James S., W. C. Mackay, and Mark Ehrman.** "Movements and Habitat Preference of Northern Pike (*Esox lucius*) in Lac Ste. Anne, Alberta." *Transaction of the American Fisheries Society* 106, 6 (1977): 560–565. Ultrasonic transmitters reveal the pike's preference for shoreline habitat and the absence of a well-defined home range—in contrast to popular opinion.

**Dobler, Elizabeth.** "Correlation between the Feeding Time of the Pike (*Esox lucius*) and the Dispersion of a School of *Leucaspius delineatus.*" *Oecologia* (Berl.) 27 (1977): 93–96. A fine study that shows why pike often seem to become active in the low light of late afternoon and early evening.

**Doxtater, Gary.** "Experimental Predator-Prey Relations in Small Ponds." *The Progressive Fish-Culturist* 29 (1967): 102–104. Comparative study of pike predation conducted by Indiana Department of Natural Resources.

**Eklov, Peter.** "Group Foraging versus Solitary Foraging Efficiency in Piscivorous Predators: The Perch, *Perca fluviatilis,* and Pike, *Esox lucius,* Patterns." *Animal Behaviour* 44 (1992): 313–326. An interesting comparison of predation strategies.

**Engels, Victor.** *Fishing in the Adirondacks in the 1930s.* Syracuse, N.Y.: Syracuse University Press, 1978. Wonderful tales of fishing for pike in the land of trout.

**Flack, Frank,** wildlife biologist, New York State Department of Conservation, pers. comm. January 1999.

*Field & Stream.* Various issues, 1920–present.

*Fly Fish America.* Various issues, 1997–present.

*Fly Fisherman.* Various issues, 1972–present.

***Fly Fishing Quarterly.*** Various issues, 1985–present.

***Fly Rod & Reel.*** Various issues, 1980–present, including some when *Rod & Reel.*

**Frost, Winifred E.** "The Food of Pike, *Esox Lucius L.,* in Windermere." *Journal of Animal Ecology* 23 (1954): 339–360. A comprehensive study (3,000 pike stomachs) that concludes abundance and availability determine species eaten by pike.

**Googland, R., D. Morris, and N. Tinbergen.** "The Spines of Sticklebacks (*Gasterosteus* and *Pygosteus*) as a Means of Defense against Predators (*Perca* and *Esox*)." *Behaviour* 10 (1957): 205–236. Concludes that pike avoid sticklebacks due to spines.

**Gustafson, Paul.** *How to Catch Bigger Pike from Rivers, Lochs, and Lakes.* London: CollinsWillow, 1997. Nicely written, beautifully illustrated book on the British method.

**Hall, D. J., and E. E. Werner.** "Seasonal Distribution and Abundance of Fishes in the Littoral Zone of a Michigan Lake." *Transactions of the American Fisheries Society* 106 (1977): 545–555. Segregation of fish species as season wears on.

**Harrison, Edward J., and Wayne F. Hadley.** "Biology of the Northern Pike in the Upper Niagara River Watershed." *New York Fish and Game Journal* 30, 1 (January 1983): 57–66. Portrayal of a marginal population.

**Hart, Paul, and Stellan F. Hamrin.** "Pike as a Selective Predator. Effects of Prey Size, Availability, Cover, and Jaw Dimensions." *Oikos,* Copenhagen 51 (1988): 220–226. Explains differences in pike as selective feeders in aquaria and opportunistic feeders in natural settings; also discusses reasons big pike utilize small prey.

**Hassler, Thomas J.** "Environmental Influences on Early Development and Year-Class Strength of Northern Pike in Lakes Oahe and Sharpe, South Dakota." *Transactions of the American Fisheries Society* 2 (1970): 369–375. Evidence for the importance of warm temperatures, high clear water, and late spawning.

**Helfman, Gene S.** "The Advantage to Fishes of Hovering in Shade." *Copeia* 2 (1981): 392–400. A terrific study on the role of shade in predation for all gamefish.

**Hoffman, Richard C.** "The Protohistory of Pike in Western Culture." In *An Annotated Bibliography of the Pike,* Esox lucius *(Osteichthyes: Salmoniformes),* E. J.

Crossman and J. M. Casselman, eds. Toronto: Royal Ontario Museum Publications in Life Sciences, 1987. A sharp, insightful, concise essay on the cultural and social history of pike fishing in Europe.

**Holschlag, Tim.** *Stream Smallmouth Fishing.* Harrisburg, Penn.: Stackpole, 1990. An excellent book on stream fishing, it contains only a brief section on pike. But the information is solid, and the topic—pike in streams—is virtually untouched anywhere else.

**Hunt, Burton P., and William F. Carbine.** "Food of Young Pike, *Esox Lucius L.,* and Associated Fishes in Peterson's Ditches, Houghton Lake, Michigan." *Transactions of the American Fisheries Society* 80 (1951): 67–84. Cites importance of predation by perch and cannibalism as important factors in mortality of young pike. Also provides overview of how diet changes with growth.

**Hunt, Robert L.** "Food of Northern Pike in a Wisconsin Trout Stream." *Transactions of the American Fisheries Society* 94 (1965): 95–97. Pike as opportunistic feeder. Also, shows rainbows to be more vulnerable to pike predation than brown trout, which have better avoidance strategies, probably.

**Hurley, D. A., and W. J. Christie.** "Depreciation of the Warmwater Fish Community in the Bay of Quinte Lake Ontario." *Journal of the Fisheries Research Board of Canada.* 34 (1977): 1849–1860. How environmental changes influence pike populations over time.

**Huver, C. W.** "Occurrence of a Northern Pike in Fisher's Island Sound." *New York Fish and Game Journal* 12, 1 (1960): 113. A pike was caught in the Atlantic Ocean nearly 20 miles from the mouth of the Connecticut River.

*In-Fisherman.* Various issues, 1980–present.

**Inskip, Peter D., and John J. Magnuson.** "Changes in Fish Populations over an 80-Year period: Big Pine Lake, Wisconsin." *Transactions of the American Fisheries Society* 112 (1983): 378–389. An interesting longitudinal look at how pike can successfully displace muskellunge.

**Janes, Edward C., ed.** *Fishing with Ray Bergman.* New York: Knopf, 1970. Includes a chapter on pike fishing.

**Johnson, Paul C.** *The Scientific Angler.* New York: Charles Scribner's Sons: 1984. Some useful information on how fish respond to artificial lures and atmospheric changes.

**LaPan, Steve,** wildlife biologist, New York State Department of Conservation, pers. comm., January 1999.

**Lawler, G. H.** "The Food of the Pike, *Esox lucius,* in Heming Lake, Manitoba." *Journal of the Fisheries Research Board of Canada* 22 (1965): 1357–1377. A very important 12-year study that examined the stomach contents of nearly 30,000 pike. Most empty stomachs in summer and among deep-water pike. Evidence for peak feeding correlating with abundance of prey. Also, discussion of bigger pike feeding on smaller pike at beginning stages of rotenone poisoning.

**Linder, Al, et al.** *Northern Pike Secrets.* Brainerd, Minn.: In-Fisherman, Inc. An absolutely invaluable book that details the seasonal patterns of pike and how to adjust tactics to fit situation. Excellent information on how pike location changes with season.

**MacLeish, William H.** *The Day Before America.* New York: Houghton Mifflin, 1994. Information on prehistory, North American–style.

**Mathis, Alicia, and Jan Smith.** "Fathead Minnows, *Pimephales promelas,* Learn to Recognize Northern Pike, *Esox lucius,* as Predators on the Basis of Chemical Stimuli from Minnows in the Pike's Diet." *Animal Behaviour* 46 (1993): 645–656. Shows how certain minnows can "sense" a pike's presence, even though the northern remains well hidden in the weeds.

**Mauck, Wilbur, and Daniel W. Coble.** "Vulnerability of Some Fishes to Northern Pike (*Esox lucius*) Predation." Journal of Fisheries Research Board of Canada 28, 7 (1971): 957–968. A very important study on pike selectivity. They aren't. There is evidence of certain prey species being more vulnerable than other species, but that has more to do with availability and vulnerability than with any sort of selectivity on the pike's part.

**McClane, A. J.** *A. J. McClane's New Standard Fishing Encyclopedia and International Angling Guide.* New York: Holt, Rinehart & Winston, 1974. Information on pike biology and how-to.

**McClane, A. J., and Keith Gardner.** *McClane's Game Fish of North America.* New York: Times Books, 1984. Nicely written species profile of pike, with where-to and how-to information.

**McNally, Tom.** *Fisherman's Bible.* Chicago: Follet, 1970. Great information from a real pike fisherman.

**Melner, Samuel, and Hermann Kessler, eds.** *Great Fishing Tackle Catalogs of the Golden Age.* New York: The Lyons Press, 1999. Shows the evolution of pike lures in the 19th and early 20th centuries.

**Moody, Robert C., John M. Helland, and Roy A. Stein.** "Escape Tactics Used by Bluegills and Fathead Minnows to Avoid Predation by Tiger Muskellunge." *Environmental Biology of Fishes* 8 (1983): 61–65. Excellent overview of how bluegills are more successful at avoiding esocid predation than are cyprinids.

*National Sportsman.* Various issues.

*New York Sportsman.* Various issues, 1983–present.

**Nilsson, P. Anders, Christer Bronmark, and Lars B. Pettersson.** "Benefits of a Predator-Induced Morphology in Crucian Carp." *Oecologia* 104 (1995): 291–296. This study offers some interesting information on pike preferences, suggesting that pike eat what they can get, but that handling time may be more with deep-bodied prey and that this may result in a preference for thin-bodied prey (at least among smaller pike). It is not possible, from my information, to decipher whether *preference* means "attacks" or "successful attacks," which means a world of difference for those of us interested in angling.

**Oppel, Frank.** *Fishing in North America 1876–1910.* Secaucus, N.J.: Castle, 1986. A rich selection of fishing articles from the past.

*Outdoor Life.* Various issues, 1920–present.

**Page, Lawrence M., and Brooks M. Burr.** *The Peterson Field Guides: A Field Guide to Freshwater Fish.* Boston: Houghton Mifflin, 1991. An excellent guide for identifying baitfish.

**Parsons, Allen P.** *Complete Book of Freshwater Fishing.* New York: Harper & Row, 1963. A chapter on pike. Mostly interesting in how it reflects the pike's midcentury niche in North America's fishery.

**Reynolds, Barry, and John Berryman.** *Pike on the Fly.* Boulder, Colo.: Johnson Books, 1993. A path-breaking book on fly fishing for northerns, with numerous fly patterns and overview of gear needed. Particularly helpful on fly fishing western reservoirs and wilderness Canadian lakes.

**Riemens, R. G.** "Survival of Northern Pike Captured by Angling and Released Immediately After Capture." *Annual Report Organisatie ter Verbetering van de Binnenvisserij* 1975/1976: 67–83. In Dutch with an English summary.

**Sammons, Steven M., Charles G. Scalet, and Robert M. Newmann.** "Seasonal and Size-Related Changes in the Diet of Northern Pike from a Shallow Prairie Lake." *Journal of Freshwater Ecology* 9, 4 (1994): 321–328. A fascinating study of the seasonal changes in pike diet in a shallow prairie reservoir, most notably the shift to leopard frogs during fall migration, small crappies during first ice, emphasizing once again the pike's tendency for taking what is available—though when it comes to centrarchids they have a propensity for the smallest available. Also suggests that ice cover enhances water clarity, leading to an increase in pike foraging.

**Schiavonne, Al,** wildlife biologist, New York State Department of Conservation, pers. comm., January 1999.

**Schullery, Paul.** *American Fly Fishing: A History.* New York: The Lyons Press, 1987. Overview of the history of pike fly fishing.

**Smith, Genio.** *Fishing in American Waters.* New York: Harper, 1869. Great early impressions of pike fishing in America.

**Smith, Harold.** *Collector's Guide to Creek Chub Lures & Collectibles.* Paducah, KY: Shroeder Publishing Co., Inc., 1997. Everything you could possibly want to know about the people behind the half century of Creek Chub lures. Beautiful photographs of lures.

**Solman, V. E. F.** "The Ecological Relations of Pike, *Esox lucius L.,* and Waterfowl." *Ecology* 26 (1945): 157–170. Interesting assessment of pike as waterfowl predator.

*Sports Afield.* Various issues, 1922–present.

**Stephenson, S. A., and W. T. Momot.** "Food Habits and Growth of Walleye, *Stizostedion vitreum,* Smallmouth Bass, *Micropterus dolomieui,* and Northern Pike, *Esox lucius,* in the Kaministiquia River, Ontario." *The Canadian-Field Naturalist* 105 (1991): 517–521. Information on feeding habits.

**Stewart, Richard.** *Bass Flies.* Intervale, N.H.: Northland Press, 1989. A well-illustrated, clearly written description of useful flies. Includes picture of and recipe for Li'l Pickerel.

**Stewart, Richard, and Farrow Allen.** *Flies for Bass and Panfish.* Intervale, N.H.: Northland Press, 1992. Part of series of fly-tying books on various species of fish. Exceptional photos and comprehensive list.

**Sternberg, Richard.** *Northern Pike and Muskies*. Minnetonka, Minn.: Cy DeCosse, Inc., 1992. Well-written, authoritative look at pike. Beautifully illustrated. Particularly helpful in overall look at North American fishery.

**Szendrey, Thomas A., and David H. Wahl.** "Effect of Feeding Experience on Growth, Vulnerability to Predation, and Survival of Esocids." *North American Journal of Fisheries Management* 15 (1995): 610–620. Information how pike diet may help provide effective coloration. Pellet-fed fingerlings had a lighter color and were perhaps more vulnerable to predation from largemouth bass as a result.

**Tapply, H. G.** *The Sportsman's Notebook*. New York: Holt, Rinehart & Winston, 1964. An elegantly written, insightful, eminently useful book on all facets of the outdoors. For pike, see in particular "Fishing with a Stripteaser."

*The Fisherman,* New England edition. Various issues, 1981–present.

**Toth, Michael.** *Freshwater Fishing Boats*. New York: Hearst Marine Books, 1995. An excellent overview of fishing boats.

**Tyus, Harold M., and James M. Beard.** "*Esox Lucius* (Esocidae) and *Stizostedion Vitreum* (Percidae) in the Green River Basin, Colorado and Utah." *Great Basin Naturalist* 50, 1 (1990): 33–39. Reveals how pike can spread through a watershed.

**Verheijen, F. J., and H. J. Reuter.** "The Effect of Alarm Substance on Predation among Cyprinids." *Animal Behavior* 17 (3): 551–554, 1969.

**Wahl, David H., and Roy A. Stein.** "Selective Predation by Three Esocids: The Role of Prey Behavior and Morphology." *Transactions of the American Fisheries Society* 117: 142–151, 1988. One of the most important studies I encountered, clearly written and well argued. The experiment revealed that pike prefer shad to bluegills—but what that means in layperson's terms is that they caught more of them, not chased more of them, which is the important notion for anglers.

*Warmwater Fly Fishing*. Various issues, 1996–present.

**Waterman, Charles F.** *A History of Angling*. Tulsa: Winchester Press, 1981. Delightful overview of angling history.

———. *Black Bass & the Fly Rod*. Harrisburg, Penn.: Stackpole, 1993. A chapter on fly fishing for northerns.

**Webb, P. W., and J. M. Skadsen.** "Strike Tactics of *Esox.*" *Canadian Journal of Zoology* 58 (1980): 1462–1469. A very interesting portrayal of how pike strike.

***Waterwolf.*** This 30-page quarterly newsletter is published exclusively for members of Pikemasters. It is filled with very useful pike-fishing material, written by some of the top pike fishermen on the continent. It offers the most practical and useful how-to, where-to, and conservation information you can find on pike. A year membership costs about as much as a crankbait (under $10). For more information, contact Pikemasters, P.O. Box 414, Marshall, MI 49068.

**Wydoski, R. S.** "Relation of Hooking Mortality and Sublethal Hooking Stress to Quality Fishery Management." In Barhart, R. A., and T. D. Roelofs, eds., *National Symposium on Catch and Release Fishing.* Humboldt State University, 43–87.

# Index